The
Dark
Night

Anne —

May the gifts of God
be yours.

Dan Schrock

The Dark Night

A GIFT OF GOD

Daniel P. Schrock

Herald Press
Scottdale, Pennsylvania
Waterloo, Ontario

Library of Congress Cataloging-in-Publication Data

Schrock, Daniel P., 1959-
  The dark night : a gift of God / by Daniel P. Schrock.
     p. cm.
  Includes bibliographical references.
  ISBN 978-0-8361-9425-8 (pbk. : alk. paper)
  1. Hidden God. 2. Spirituality. I. Title.
  BT180.H54S37 2008
  248.2–dc22
                                    2008033639

THE DARK NIGHT
Copyright © 2009 by Herald Press, Scottdale, Pa. 15683
    Published simultaneously in Canada by Herald Press,
    Waterloo, Ont. N2L 6H7. All rights reserved
International Standard Book Number: 978-0-8361-9425-8
Library of Congress Catalog Card Number: 2008033639
Printed in the United States of America
Book design by Joshua Byler
Cover by Sans Serif

13 12 11 10 09   10 9 8 7 6 5 4 3 2 1

To order or request information please call 1-800-245-7894
or visit www.heraldpress.com.

In gratitude to the people in the congregations I have served:
Lombard Mennonite
Columbus Mennonite
Berkey Avenue Mennonite

God is an ocean
God is an anchor
and God is a sail
At times I'm floating in God
flowing with the ebbs and undertows
and sometimes God holds me where I am
in spite of all-encompassing currents
and other times God pulls me
through bright days
and dark nights
and my friends' dark nights
God saves me from drowning
and I wish to drown in God's love

God is a storm
and God is a rocky mountain peak
on which I lie exposed
and vulnerable
sometimes wishing for lightning
sometimes hoping for peace

And after all this
God is a hammer
and a nail
and a plan.
I hope we do good work.

Dan Eisenstat, May 22, 2005
    Statement of Faith upon the occasion of his baptism

CONTENTS

Part 4: The Night's Conversions

FOREWORD

When Menno Simons died in 1561, John of the Cross was only nineteen years old and still a student at the local Jesuit college in Medina del Campo, Spain. The paths of these two religiously committed young men never crossed. However, four centuries later pastor Daniel P. Schrock has brought to the attention of his Mennonite tradition the teachings on the dark night as originally articulated by John of the Cross in his poem and its commentary known as *The Dark Night*. Is not the convergence in our time of these two sixteenth-century religious figures a sign of ecumenical progress at a moment when we sorely need to find ways to share with each other the riches of our differing traditions? As we do so, we ally ourselves with the prayer of Jesus that we may all be one (see John 17:20). Schrock's book is not a study of John of the Cross; yet, Schrock's *The Dark Night* takes its title and inspiration from the Spanish poet, and one senses John's loving and wise presence throughout this book. It is evident that the teachings of John of the Cross have made a deep impression on this beloved Mennonite pastor.

John's poem celebrates how God's love transforms one into a new person in Christ through the dark suffering that occurs as one grows spiritually. John, a Carmelite friar, used the metaphor of dark night to describe the transition from meditation to deeply graced prayer. Schrock has astutely and with great pastoral sensitivity applied the metaphor to the spiritual lives of contemporary Christians who encounter darkness and suffering in what Elizabeth Johnson calls their "quest for the living God."

Schrock is a gifted pastor and spiritual guide who has gained rich insights into what occurs as one lives seriously the Christian life of prayer and service. As he knows from his studies and his experience as a pastor and confidant, Schrock has learned much about the darkness that often descends on one in varying degrees and intensity as one grows as a disciple of Jesus Christ. In this book he shares what he has discovered about the darkness that descends like a disturbing shadow over the spiritual life of those who have passed beyond the beginning stage of the Christian walk. This initial stage is a time when one's enthusiasm for the Lord dominates one's feelings. The dark night is a process of maturation, a time to become a more loving Christian.

One never has to guess what Schrock means as he explores the dark night. He is always clear, and he writes with a fresh, engaging, and even passionate style. Moreover, Schrock wears his wisdom lightly. He has a profound respect for those whom he pastors; warmth for his readers permeates every page of this book. I suspect that many readers will pause to mull over the wisdom distilled so diligently by a very experienced spiritual guide.

In the preface, Schrock acknowledges the inspiration of John of the Cross on his own spiritual life. Then he moves on in the book to present spiritual guidance in a lively contemporary idiom that foregoes explicit mention of John's language and categories. So in the brief pages of this foreword, I want to sample some of John's explicit convictions about darkness and love as the destiny of all Christians. First of all, John was convinced that the dark night always occurs for the sake of light and love. Keeping that wisdom in mind enables one to live with a sturdy hope even in the darkest of nights. John also recommends that "where there is no love, put love and you will draw out love," and "the soul lives where she loves." Finally, John tells those whom he guides that "in the evening of life you will be examined in love." John of the Cross is all about love. Dan's book investigates how Christians can navigate the spiritual life's dark waters so that they may live life to the full with the love of God.

John of the Cross discovered that the dark night is a reflection of God's providential guiding. It is an experience in which God "speaks in the night" and in which God draws ever closer to the human heart. John was a gifted poet who described the dark night in its paradoxical transition from meditation to gifted prayer with these lines, the wisdom of which is easily detected in Schrock's lively and inspiring prose.

> O guiding night!
> O night more lovely than the dawn!

For the John of the Cross, the experience of the dark night was all about growing in the love of God. Dan Schrock's sensitive and caring direction is rooted in the same inspiration that shaped John's teaching: "'You shall love the Lord your God with all your heart, and with all your soul, and with all your mind, and with all your strength.' The second is this, 'You shall love your neighbor as yourself'" (Mark 12:30-31). The Father raised Jesus Christ in a blaze of glory after his darkest hour on the cross; the Father will raise to newness of life everyone who remains faithful no matter the darkness in which one may be engulfed. God's love is always nearby, within the darkness and just on the other side of darkness.

Keith J. Egan
Carmelite Institute
Washington, D.C.

PREFACE

Who among you fears the LORD
    and obeys the voice of his servant,
who walks in darkness
    and has no light,
yet trusts in the name of the LORD
    and relies upon his God?
                —Isaiah 50:10

I did not want to have anything to do with the dark night of the soul. In particular, I did not want to go through it.

I grew up in the Mennonite church and had never heard of what I call in this book "the dark night." I heard plenty about conversion, discipleship, suffering, hell, and heaven. No one told me that God gives the dark night to many Christians or that at any point in time some people in nearly every congregation are living inside a dark night. Certainly no one helped me to understand that the dark night, contrary to what we might think, is actually a wonderful gift from God.

I first encountered the idea of the dark night in a little book given to me as a present when I graduated from college, Thomas Merton's *Contemplative Prayer*. That slim volume and a Bible were the only books I took with me after graduation when I flew to Tegucigalpa, Honduras, to live for three months among that country's generous people. In the context of poverty greater than I had ever seen and of a culture I struggled to understand, I tried to comprehend what Merton was talking about. I was not very successful. With my evangelical Mennonite background, I was not familiar with many of the key words Merton used, words like *meditation, contemplation,* and *detachment.*

I persisted to the end of the book, largely out of respect for the people who had given it to me. Paul and Ann Gingrich combined between them much of what I have been trying to imitate ever since: a passion for mission, conversion, service to Christ and his church, and spiritual care for others. I respected them highly (and still do), but I could not figure out why they gave me a book that was so unlike anything I had read before. Why give a book birthed in a Catholic monastery to a young Mennonite who grew up in a small mission church on the edge of a poor, white Appalachian community?

Whatever Ann and Paul had in mind with their gift, it was a turning point and led circuitously to the book you hold in your hands. In the fourth chapter of *Contemplative Prayer*, Merton writes about "the night of the senses," and in the next chapter about "the dark night" and "the night of pure faith."[1] I had no idea what he was talking about, but I knew that this business about the night sounded awful and that under no circumstances did I want to experience it. Little did I perceive, sitting there with Merton in Tegucigalpa, that I had already experienced the dark night—twice.

Nine years later I became a pastor. Soon I began noticing a mysterious spiritual phenomenon in some members of my congregation. This odd phenomenon, whatever it was, flickered at the edges of conversation in my one-on-one meetings with parishioners. These followers of Christ appeared to be dispirited, as if they had just lost their best friend. They said they felt disconnected from God, even though they were doing all the right things to nurture their relationship to Christ and the church; they prayed, studied the Bible, worshipped, and served others. I knew them well enough (or thought I did) to guess that neither depression nor unconfessed sin was the source of their trouble. If the trouble wasn't spiritual laziness, depression, or sin, what was it? Why did they look dried up, as if the juice of living had been squeezed from them?

By 1998, the same mysterious phenomenon had taken up residence in my own life (or as I would later realize, had again taken up residence). God, whom I imagined hovering less than three feet away from me during the early years of my pastoral work, moved about a hundred feet away and sat down to watch what I would do in response. God was not absent, exactly, just distant—more distant than I wanted God to be. "Why did you move?" I asked, "or was it I who moved?"

I searched myself anxiously, looking for some instance of new sin that might have pushed God away. There was plenty of sin there, to be sure, but it was old sin that had been around a long time. Nothing new. Nor had I slacked off in any of my spiritual practices of prayer, Bible study, worship, and service. In fact, I kept all those and had recently added some new spiritual practices. Clinical depression did not seem like the right diagnosis; I was highly energetic both at work and at home. Moreover there was no other crisis in my life, no illness, no death, and no difficulty at work. Things at the church were actually better than ever before.

At about that time I changed spiritual directors. After listening to me once a month for half a year, this new director said near the end of our session, "Dan, I think what's going on in you is the dark night of the soul, specifically the dark night of the senses. If you're interested in finding out more about that, I suggest you read book one of *The Dark Night*, by John of the Cross. That's the first and best description anywhere of what I think is happening to you—the dark night. If you're interested, why don't you read it and see what you think?"

It was as if he had switched on a krypton flashlight and aimed it at the thing that had been hiding in the shadows of the room. Back in seminary, I had mucked around enough in spiritual theology (sometimes called mystical theology) to know in simple terms what the dark night was. I realized that the mysterious phenomenon I was seeing in others, and now in myself, was probably a dark night.

Since then I've tried to understand the dark night and how it expresses itself in the lives of ordinary followers of Jesus. This quest has taken me through scores of books, led me to interview dozens of people who are or were in a dark night, and taken me back to school to study the biblical, theological, and historical expressions of the dark night from some outstanding teachers.

The person who coined the phrase "dark night" was John of the Cross, a sixteenth-century Spanish Carmelite poet and spiritual guide.[2] In the centuries before John, medieval theologians such as Gregory of Nyssa, Pseudo-Dionysius the Areopagite, Johannes Tauler, and Jan van Ruysbroeck explored the relationship between God and darkness, taking their cue from biblical passages such as Psalm 18:11 and Isaiah 45:7. In fourteenth-century England, an anonymous monk wrote *The Cloud of Unknowing* and *The Book of Privy Counsel*, which describe what John of the Cross would call two centuries later the "night of sense" and the "night of spirit."

But it was John who invented the term *la noche oscura*, usually translated as "the dark night." This phrase can also be translated as "the obscure night"—an apt term because the experience feels so obscure and confusing.[3] In fourteen poems, four commentaries, and other assorted works, John wrote in detail about why God leads us into the night and how God changes us through it. John's observations are so compelling that anyone who wants to write about the dark night, even four centuries later, must rely on him. This book owes much to him. But John's writings are neither readily available in libraries nor easy to read, so I have chosen not to refer explicitly to him, except in this preface.

The dark night is a metaphor for one of the ways God shapes us more fully into the image of Christ, using the tools of divine light and love. The dark night helps us to flourish as followers of Christ. According to John, three signs indicate a dark night, and for the experience to be an authentic dark night, all three signs must be present at the same time: first, a sense of dryness in one's spiritual life; second, a difficult time praying in one's usual way, sometimes even an inability to pray; and third, a growing desire to be alone in loving awareness of God.[4]

∽

The experience of the dark night is at least as old as the Bible, even though no biblical text uses the phrase *dark night* or fully describes it, something that is also true for the doctrine of the Trinity. No biblical writer uses *Trinity* or *triune* God, and no passage succinctly lays out the creedal affirmation that God exists eternally in three persons as Father, Son, and Holy Spirit. Instead, the theology of the Trinity is constructed with many different biblical texts using human reason and experience. This also holds true for many of the church's other theological affirmations, including the dark night. Using the Bible, reason, and experience, the dark night is a theological construct that helps us understand a pattern of interactions that God uses to extend the new creation within us (see 2 Corinthians 5:17).

People might squirm at the idea that an experience of obscurity and apparent darkness can be an avenue for God's new creation. After all, 1 John 1:5 asserts that "God is light and in him there is no darkness at all." True enough. Darkness is not in God, but God acts in the darkness. Throughout the Bible, many of God's most creative, salvific actions occur at night, in the context of obscure darkness. This includes the creation of the world; the formation of a chosen people; the exodus from Egypt; and the birth, arrest, crucifixion, and resurrection of Jesus. Throughout the Bible, darkness is a crucible in which God creates and re-creates shalom for the world. In the night, God forms relationships with us, liberates us from injustice, and saves us. In short, God converts us during the night.[5]

Readers familiar with John of the Cross will notice that I do not distinguish the night of sense from the night of spirit. For John, the night of sense happens to many Christians and begins to purify the sensory part of the human being; the night of spirit happens to fewer Christians and purifies the spiritual part of the human being. It is a far more intense experience of inner suffering than the night of sense.

I have four reasons for not pursuing John's distinction between the nights of sense and spirit in this book. First, the distinction between sense and spirit reflects medieval psychology as well as his scholastic training at the University of Salamanca, but it does not fit well with the modern understanding of the human person as an integrated whole.[6]

Second, John does not designate specific signs for discerning the night of the spirit, as he does for discerning the night of the senses. His lack of separate criteria for identifying the night of the spirit implies that it is largely an intensification of the night of the senses, rather than a discrete phenomenon.

Third, only the night of spirit achieves the final purification of the senses,[7] which makes it difficult to determine whether someone's night is happening purely in the senses, purely in the spirit, or concurrently in both spirit and senses. A person may first experience the night of sense and later the night of spirit, at other times may alternate back and forth between them, or at other times may experience both simultaneously. God may even reverse them so that we go through the night of spirit first and the night of sense second.[8]

Fourth, John insists that we are "one suppositum," just as the triune God is one suppositum.[9] In other words, the human person is a unity of various parts as God is a unity of three persons.

John's methodology reflects this conviction when in book one of his *Dark Night* commentary he uses the first stanza of "The Dark Night" poem to discuss the night of sense, and then in book two begins all over again with the poem's first stanza to discuss the night of spirit. In the literary world created by the poem, all events—whether they are of sense or spirit—happen during the same night rather than during multiple nights.

The Structure of This Book

This book has four sections. The first begins with Jesus and our call to follow him. In what way did Jesus experience Godforsakenness? How might our conversion lead to cruciform living? The second section discusses the dark night's dynamics. How does the dark night fit into some of the other spiritual movements in our lives, and what is God trying to accomplish by giving us this experience? The third explores the night's appearances in differing arenas of life. How might it unfold in vocation, in family life, and in groups such as congregations? The fourth speaks of the night's conversions. How does the night change us? In what new ways are we released for discipleship and mission?

Over the years, many people have honored me by sharing in confidence their experiences of living through the dark night. Out of respect for confidentiality, the case studies in this book are drawn from bits and pieces of various people's lives. I'm not obligated to keep my own stories confidential, so those really happened as written. I pray that in small ways this volume will help ordinary Christians understand the frustrating yet wonderful gift that God, in mercy and love, has chosen to give them—the dark night.

Acknowledgments

I am grateful for the help of many people. The members of Columbus Mennonite Church, Columbus, Ohio, responded kindly to my earliest sermons on the dark night, while the members of Berkey Avenue Mennonite Fellowship, Goshen, Indiana, graciously listened to further sermons on the dark night, challenged me during an adult Christian education class on the topic, and then gave me a sabbatical to write an early draft of this book.

By their warmth, Rick and Robin Dietrich redefined for me the meaning of Christian hospitality. Late one night while staying in their home, I hatched the mad idea of focusing my doctoral work on the dark night. Although this is not quite the book he had in mind, John D. Roth encouraged me to begin and shaped some of the overarching ideas. Anita Kehr thoughtfully inquired how things were going and made a few crucial observations. For reading drafts, pointing out problems, and suggesting numerous improvements, I am most grateful to Marcus Smucker, Jennifer Schrock, and Evan Bontrager. Along the way, Richard Sweeney, Thomas Kapacinskas, and Dwight Judy have provided excellent and insightful guidance. Keith Egan spent many hours, both in his home and in the classroom, guiding me through John of the Cross. Dozens of women and men from a wide variety of cultural, economic, and religious backgrounds have willingly told me in detail about their own dark nights. To all of these, my heartfelt thanks.

—Daniel P. Schrock

Part 1

JESUS AND THE CALL TO FOLLOW

— 1 —

JESUS' GODFORSAKENNESS

> When it was noon, darkness came over the whole land
> until three in the afternoon. At three o'clock Jesus cried out
> with a loud voice, "Eloi, Eloi, lema sabachthani?" which
> means, "My God, my God, why have you forsaken me?"
>   When some of the bystanders heard it, they said, "Listen,
> he is calling for Elijah." And someone ran, filled a sponge
> with sour wine, put it on a stick, and gave it to him to drink,
> saying, "Wait, let us see whether Elijah will come to take
> him down." Then Jesus gave a loud cry and breathed his last.
>   —Mark 15:33-37

When Jesus died, he thought God had abandoned him. The
only prayer his desolate soul could utter was an unanswered
question: "My God, my God, why have you forsaken me?"

Jesus' relationship with God did not start out this way.
From the day of his baptism in the Jordan River as an adult,
Jesus enjoyed an intimate relationship with God that gave him
a sense of being called, blessed, and sustained. Immediately after

coming up out of the Jordan, he saw the door of heaven thrust open, watched the Holy Spirit fly out toward him, felt the Spirit's soft wings brush his cheeks, and heard a voice booming from heaven's doorway: "You are my Son, the Beloved; with you I am well pleased" (Mark 1:11).

Until Jesus came to the cross, this visceral sense of the Holy Spirit's presence apparently never left him. Jesus saw visible proof of the Spirit's nearness throughout his public ministry. How else but through the Spirit could he have confronted demons and won (see 1:21-27)? How else could he have healed scabby skin and made it soft, smooth, and supple like a baby's, except by the Holy Spirit (see 1:40-42)? How else could he have halted a storm in its tracks (see 4:35-41), stirred up life in a dead twelve-year-old girl (see 5:35-42), and broken five loaves and two fish into enough pieces to treat five thousand men plus an uncounted number of women and children to a feast (see 6:38-44)? Each time Jesus performed one of these wonderful signs, it verified again that he worked in cooperation with God's own Spirit. Jesus and the Spirit were like foot to a sandal, like words to a song.

In addition to the dramatic healings and feedings that convinced Jesus that the Holy Spirit hovered nearby, there was also that strange experience on a high mountain that later generations call the transfiguration (see 9:2-8). Jesus' clothes were made luminously white; he had a heart-to-heart chat with Elijah and Moses; and again he heard that voice from the cloud of heaven: "This is my Son, the Beloved; listen to him!" (verse 7). What clearer indication of God's nearness, blessing, and care could he want than that?

Jesus' private prayer life was gratifying too. Early in Mark's Gospel, we see Jesus seeking silence and solitude: "In the morning, while it was still very dark, he got up and went out to a deserted place, and there he prayed" (1:35). Before sunrise, he arose from bed and walked to a deserted location away from all distractions, where he prayed alone and in silence with only creation around him. On another occasion he again left everyone behind and hiked up a local mountain to pray (see 6:46). Although we do not know the content of Jesus' prayers, we do know he sometimes addressed God with the Aramaic word *Abba*, meaning "Daddy," which infers that he and God enjoyed a high level of closeness and trust (see 14:36).

Jesus knew that God loved him, claimed him, and worked through him. In the context of this intimate relationship, he knew what God wanted and did what God asked. Jesus eventually went to Jerusalem, where during one dark night at Gethsemane, he prayed in desperation. There his sense of intimacy with God and support from God started to disintegrate. Throwing himself on the ground in fear of his imminent arrest, trial, and crucifixion, Jesus explicitly asked God, his own daddy, to take away all the suffering that Jesus knew was heading his way (see 14:35). But he heard nothing in response. God did not answer. God sat in silence. God did not stop the unfolding course of events.

As soon as Jesus gave up this frustrating prayer, people came to arrest him, which set in motion a series of ten desertions, betrayals, and sufferings, each of which conveyed to Jesus the depth of his abandonment by others. They happened in rapid succession.

- The religious leaders of his own people hauled him off to a kangaroo court (see 14:43, 53).
- The disciples fled into hiding (see 14:50).
- Liars at the trial accused him of things he did not do (see 14:56-59).
- The priests spat on him and the guards beat him (see 14:65).
- Peter, one of Jesus' closest disciples, insisted he never knew him (see 14:66-72).
- The crowd chose to give clemency to Barabbas, an acknowledged murderer, and demanded that Pilate crucify Jesus (see 15:6-14).

- Pilate caved in to the crowd and handed Jesus over for crucifixion (see 15:15).
- Roman soldiers flogged him and mocked him (see 15:15-20).
- Both priests and passersby jeered at him (see 15:29-32).
- From nine o'clock in the morning until evening, Jesus hung on a cross in public view, stark naked (see 15:22-25, 42-43).

In other words, Jesus was abandoned by the religious leaders, his disciples, the crowds who were once so enthusiastic about him, his governor, and the local police force. He was crucified in physical agony and spiritual anguish, feeling that his own daddy had utterly forsaken him. Jesus died in something very close to a dark night.

Perhaps we could say that on the day Jesus died, a sense of forsakenness entered the heart of God. At the crucifixion, part of God felt abandoned by the other two parts of God. We should not suppose that the other two persons of the Trinity were unaffected when Jesus felt so abandoned. What happened to God the Son on that day profoundly influenced God the Father and God the Spirit. Therefore when God grants you or me a dark night, Jesus knows what it's like not to sense God's presence, what it's like to be unable to pray except in the most dire and desperate words, and what it's like not to receive comfort. Jesus already knows the absence, the dryness, and the loss.

God's Unflagging Presence

As part of our baptism, Christians pledge to follow Jesus in discipleship wherever he takes us. You and I are not likely to be physically crucified. But discipleship sometimes takes us into a dark night where we feel abandoned by God. This spiritual crucifixion brings us to the new life of resurrection. If you are currently in a dark night, remember that Jesus experienced something similar. If you have already passed through a dark night, recall that Jesus passed through something like it too. If in the future you are taken into a dark night, do not forget that Jesus has gone on ahead of you to new life. He understands better than we do what the dark night is all about.

In his dying moments Jesus thought God had forsaken him, but you and I know that God did not, and at the resurrection Jesus also knew that God did not. We know that in the death of Jesus, God vigorously engaged the world in a fresh way to further the divine mission of creating shalom, a Hebrew idea that refers to God's gift of peace and wholeness of life. We believe that the crucifixion brought God closer to us than God had ever come before. We trust that God intimately engaged us in Jesus' desolation at Golgotha. We see that in the resurrection, God vindicated the way of Jesus and created an entirely new kind of life.

As we will see more fully in later chapters, the great paradox of the dark night is that our feeling of Godforsakenness during the night, along with our passion to reconnect with God, is itself a sign of God's nearness. The abandonment we feel in a dark night is itself a sign of God's presence in a different way than we have perhaps experienced before. Our inability to pray joyfully during a dark night may be the most profound praying we have ever done, because the dark night simplifies our prayer to pure desire. Our experience of emptiness, incredible though it may sound, indicates the powerful work of God hidden deep within us. Our despair testifies to hope, and our dying prepares us for spiritual growth.

When we're in a dark night, we usually don't want to be there. But most of us also have an odd conviction that the night is just where we need to be right now, that God has led us to this place for a time, and that we are being called to love the night. This does not mean we are called to love suffering, but that we are called to love what God is doing for us in the night. We sense that important changes are happening, though we do not know what those changes are. And we are right about this odd conviction. God has led us to this experience and is working deeply in it for the purpose of transformation, light, and love.

Because the dark night is God's doing, God directs the course, length, and intensity of it. In a dark night we can do some things to respond and cooperate with God (more on this in chapter 7). But mostly we wait on God, as confusing and as hard as that sometimes is. Like Jesus, we relinquish ourselves into God's care, to wait and see what resurrection, what newness, God will accomplish next. That newness can take the most surprising forms.

—2—

EMBRACING THE CROSS

I want to know Christ and the power of his resurrection
and the sharing of his sufferings by becoming like him
in his death.

—Philippians 3:10

I was almost ready to go home after a day at the church office
when the doorbell rang. I opened the door to a man standing
on the front porch. "Are you the pastor of this church?" he asked
nervously as he snuffed out the cigarette he had been smoking
and threw the butt into the bushes. Furtively glancing up and
down the street, he said, "I need to come in. Please let me in
right now before anyone sees me. I'll explain when I'm inside."

The man standing in front of me that afternoon appeared to
be in his mid-thirties. Mixed with the odor of cigarette smoke was
the sweet smell of cologne. His eyes were clear, not bloodshot. His
breath was normal, not laced with alcohol. His fingernails,
though stained a mild yellow from cigarettes, were well mani-
cured. His clothes—ironed black designer jeans with a cream-col-

ored sport shirt and a black leather jacket—appeared to be as clean as mine, and probably a lot more expensive. His hair was immaculately styled. But about him was an air I have never detected before or since from strangers asking me for help: the air of a man afraid for his life. As soon as he came in and closed the door, he went to the window and discreetly peeked through the slats of the Venetian blind to check the street outside.

We sat down, and he told me his story. He was, he said, a member of the Mafia, descended from Sicilians who had immigrated to the United States. For many years he had done whatever his Mafia bosses told him to do. If they told him to extort money from someone, he extorted money. If they told him to threaten people, he threatened them. If they told him to kill someone, he obeyed orders. In return for unquestioning obedience, his bosses rewarded him well. He had plenty of money to buy almost any kind of clothes he wanted. He ate at the best restaurants. His favorite meal, he said with a smile, was seafood and pasta at a certain restaurant where the entrées cost fifty dollars. And if anyone got mad at him or crossed him, his bosses took care of it. Even though his work prevented him from getting married, having children, and settling down in one place, he was satisfied with his life, all in all.

He had been born into the Catholic Church, he continued, but Christianity was so peripheral to his life that it hardly mattered. Then, about three years ago, he met a pastor named Tom in one of the cities where he was working. Tom was about his own age, early thirties, with a handsome wife and two wonderful children. He and Tom became friends, and during their conversations in Tom's living room while his children played on the floor, they talked about God. There was a lot about Tom that he found attractive: a stable life, a strong marriage, delightful children, and above all, an intimate connection with God that seemed to give Tom a deep sense of peace. During those months of friendship with Tom, he thought seriously about becoming a

Christian and asking Tom to baptize him. But when his boss in the Mafia moved him to a new assignment in another location, he lost contact with Tom.

Now he was in a crisis, because last week his boss had ordered him to kill another person and get rid of the body. This time he knew he couldn't carry out the order, because his conscience would not let him. At first killing had been no problem: just do it, get rid of the body so the police would never find it, and move on to the next assignment. He hadn't actually killed all that many people, only a handful. But in the last year or two the killing was starting to get to him. Was killing people right? What did God think about killing? What did God think about the Mafia?

These doubts continued, and so for a few days he procrastinated, telling his boss he had not been able to find the person in a position where he could do the job quietly. That excuse didn't last long because the boss was suspicious that he was getting soft. So he ran, and had been running ever since, eluding the men his boss had sent to catch him. If they did catch him, they would kill *him* and dispose of *his* body without a trace. That's the choice the Mafia offers: obey orders or be killed.

But he'd had enough of killing, and he wanted out of the Mafia. He simply could not continue. He would run as long as he could, take a Greyhound bus, perhaps, and escape to the western United States, alter his appearance, forge a new identity for himself, and find a new line of work. Maybe someday he'd even get married and have children. Yet it was more likely he would die for his decision to leave the Mafia, more likely they would catch him and kill him. But so be it. He would not kill anyone else.

And he wanted to become a Christian. Could he be baptized, now, this afternoon? "I don't know how much longer I have left to live," he said, "maybe hours, maybe days, maybe weeks. I know all their tricks for finding people, but there are more of them than there are of me. I've been struggling for several years with becoming a Christian, and the time has arrived. I want to do it now. And to symbolize my new identity as a follower of Christ, I want to have a new name. I will not tell you my real name, because the less you know about the details of my life, the better, just in case you are ever questioned. I want to be baptized with the new name of Thomas in honor of that pastor who first helped me to connect with God."

As I listened I wondered if he might have schizophrenia, so incredible was his story. But when he asked for baptism, I decided that even if he did have a mental illness, I was responsible as a pastor to respond to his request at face value. The question of possible illness was irrelevant and should not prevent baptism. Next I debated whether to baptize him on the spot without the kind of extensive prebaptismal preparation I normally did with people. "Help!" I prayed. "What should I do?"

I decided to listen some more. I asked about his spiritual life and what he thought about Jesus' willingness to be killed rather than to kill someone else. His answers displayed calm understanding and genuine commitment. I realized that like my spiritual ancestors, the Anabaptists of the sixteenth century, this man was counting the cost of faith and choosing baptism to express a radical commitment to Christ. I decided to baptize him.

Thirty minutes later the two of us faced each other on our knees at the front of the sanctuary. From the Mennonite Church's *Minister's Manual*, I read him the questions of commitment, using his new name.

"Thomas, do you renounce the evil powers of this world and turn to Jesus Christ as your savior? Do you put your trust in his grace and love and promise to obey him as your Lord?"

Locking eyes with me, he nodded his head. "Yes."

"Do you believe in God, the Father Almighty, maker of heaven and earth; in Jesus Christ, God's Son, our Lord; and in the Holy Spirit, the giver of life?"

"I do."

"Do you accept the Word of God as guide and authority for your life?"

"Yes."

"Are you willing to give and receive counsel in whatever congregation you eventually join?"[10]

He nodded.

"Are you ready to participate in the mission of the church?"

"I am."

Putting my hands on his shoulders, I baptized him, the cool water cascading off his head, bouncing down his shoulders, rolling from his lap to the carpet, using the ageless words: "Thomas, upon your confession of faith in Jesus Christ, I baptize you with water in the name of the Father, the Son, and the Holy Spirit." My hands still on him, I prayed for protection, for safety, and for the gift and the power of the Spirit. I thanked God for this new saint and member of the household of God.

When we were done, I drove Thomas to the Greyhound bus station. Before he would get out of the car, he asked me to circle the station several times so he could look for signs of danger. Finally he consented to get out, fear gathering in his eyes.

I never heard from him again. I do not know if he still lives or if he is dead. But I do know that Thomas left our congregation's building changed, free from needing to kill any more people, attracted by love to follow Jesus Christ.[11]

An Invitation to Follow

[Jesus] sternly ordered and commanded them not to tell anyone, saying, "The Son of Man must undergo great suffering, and be rejected by the elders, chief priests, and scribes, and be killed, and on the third day be raised."

Then he said to them all, "If any want to become my followers, let them deny themselves and take up their cross daily and follow me. For those who want to save their life will lose it, and those who lose their life for my sake will save it." (Luke 9:21-24)

When we agree to follow Jesus, we have no idea where this journey of faith will take us. Something about Jesus attracts us or entices us to say, "Yes, I will go with you." To use the language of Psalm 23, we believe Jesus will guide us like a shepherd. The specifics, however, are unclear. In what green pastures will he invite us to lie down? What still waters will he send to restore our souls? To what dark valleys will he beckon us? What meals will he prepare for us to eat with our enemies? In which directions will his rod and staff point? How shall his goodness and mercy pursue us all the days of our lives? We do not know. The details about our future with him remain mysterious.

Yet in general we know a few things. We know, for instance, that when we commit ourselves to Jesus Christ, he in turn commits himself to us, giving us his Spirit as a sign of that commitment, which means that the same Spirit who descended upon Jesus at his baptism in the Jordan River also descends on us (see Luke 3:22; Acts 2:4). By way of the Spirit, our lives are now forever bound up with Jesus' life. His work is now our work. The shape of his life is now the shape of our lives; his patterns and priorities are now our patterns and priorities.

Suffering and Crucifixion Are Normal

If Jesus suffered and if our lives are patterned closely after Jesus', then it should not surprise us if we also suffer. On the day of his baptism, Thomas may or may not have known that Jesus urged his followers to take up their cross daily (see Mark 8:34). Yet Thomas was clearly living this verse. He knew that by leaving the Mafia to follow Christ, there was a good chance he'd be killed. Before he appeared at the door of our church, he had already grasped the simple truth that following Jesus could entail suffering and death. Although Thomas was no would-be martyr seeking death, he knew death could easily happen to him. Nevertheless he went ahead and committed himself to God in the face of possible, even likely, death.

In each synoptic Gospel, Jesus urges people who want to follow him to deny themselves and take up their cross (see Matthew 16:24; Mark 8:34; Luke 9:23). Of course we choose whether or not to follow Jesus, but once we choose to follow, the part about the cross is not optional. Following Christ does not mean that we are compelled to seek a cross, because ordinary Christian living will put enough crosses in our path without us hunting for more. Jesus does not say to seek suffering; he merely says that when the path of discipleship takes us to a cross, he would like us to pick it up and carry it. If we do so, then we will follow him to the place of crucifixion where we will die. For Christians, dying is not a choice, but an inevitable, fundamental part of the Christian faith. Christians do not necessarily suffer more than other people, but unlike others, we do have hope that God will transform our suffering. Therefore we do not need to dodge suffering and death at all costs.

This message is not popular and will not likely win millions of new converts. Even with the most savvy marketing techniques, such a message is difficult to package in a way non-Christians will want to follow Christ. Most North Americans do not want to die. At nearly any medical cost, we want to escape pain, elude suffering, and delay dying. We'd rather pursue a life of ease and luxury, grabbing as much as possible from others in the world, working hard to avoid the one physical death that all human beings will come to sooner or later—our own. So for Christians to talk about dying, whether spiritually or physically, is more than most non-Christians want to consider. As Paul wrote to the Corinthians, "The message about the cross is foolishness to those who are perishing, but to us who are being saved it is the power of God" (1 Corinthians 1:18).

One of the umpteen ways to be missional is to be evangelistic—to beckon people who demonstrate no faith in God to repent, turn their lives around, and start following Jesus. Evangelism is certainly part of the Christian gospel. But in an effort to convert as many people as possible, we have sometimes talked only about how wonderful Jesus is, only about the joy in following him, and only about the blessings of new life that come when we say yes to God.

Jesus is wonderful, we do have joy in following him, and God does bless us with new life—but these are only part of the truth. Another part of the truth is that following Jesus includes dying. Evangelism would have more integrity if, early on, we were honest with the unchurched about the possibility of spiritual death. I imagine a candid admission that might run something like this: "Look, my friend, I want you to know that if you decide to become a Christian, God will give you extensive spiritual rewards. But I also want you to know that you may end up dying in a profound way. You may end up letting go of some things you'd rather not let go of. God might lovingly but persistently detach you from many of the things you think you can't live without—from some of your fondest dreams, your most valued projects, and your favorite pleasures. The Christian life includes the possibility of spiritual crucifixion. Along the way you will have joy, love, and peace; but, to be honest, your commitment may also lead you into darkness, dryness, and death."

Not often have I heard Christians talk this way. I once took a class on Christian ethics. Before the class began, the professor emailed us several assignments, one of which was to write down the virtues that we thought Christians should have. When we gathered for the opening days of class, she asked us to list all these virtues on the chalkboard at the front of the room. By the time we were done, we had a long and impressive list of perhaps thirty or forty virtues—things like hope, love, courage, peace, reverence, joy, and integrity. Our professor carefully looked at the list, and then made a crucial observation: "All those virtues you've listed are virtues anybody could practice, even non-Christians. A Christian might practice love or reverence or integrity better than a non-Christian, but a non-Christian could live out all those virtues—with one exception. One of you wrote on the board *cruciformity*. That's a specifically Christian virtue that non-Christians cannot really practice."

Cruciformity well captures what Jesus means by taking up our cross daily. *Cruciform* means anything shaped like a cross: in church architecture, a cruciform floor plan is laid out in the shape of a cross. Jesus infers that the Christian life is by nature cruciform—that your life and mine are formed in the pattern of a cross. After years of carrying crosses, our life itself becomes like a cross. The virtue of cruciformity is therefore the pursuit of cruciform living. As we open ourselves more fully to God and others, our lives are remade into a cross, and it is this dying—along with the new life that follows—that makes Christian spirituality distinctively Christian.

The dark night—a sense of inner dryness, an inability to pray in the usual way, and a growing desire to be alone in loving attention to God—is one way we might undergo an inner spiritual crucifixion. It's a way God shapes our lives to be cruciform. Parts of us die to Christ while other parts rise to new life.

True Self and False Self

One way to understand which parts of us die and which parts of us rise to newness is to think of a true self and a false self. The Bible nowhere uses the phrases *true self* and *false self*. Yet we find similar language in Romans 7:14-25, where Paul writes about the "I" who struggles with a tension between the "law of God" and the "law of sin" (verse 25). This I wants to do good, yet at the same time does evil: "For I do not do what I want, but I do the very thing I hate. . . . I do not do the good I want, but the evil I do not want is what I do" (verses 15b, 19). This describes our dilemma well. At different times we are variously inclined to evil and sin or to holiness and goodness.

Our true self—the part that delights in the law of God—was created by God at our birth and carries the imprint of the divine image (see Genesis 1:26). It is our best self, gladly basking in the presence of God, longing for obedience to the ways of God, and genuinely wanting to live in communion with God. By contrast, our false self—the part that is bound to the law of sin—moves in a direction going away from God. For my new friend Thomas, the false self had become dominant. Through the act of conversion and baptism, he signaled his desire for that false self to wither and his true self to flourish by God's mercy.

The false self starts to take shape when we are children. We shape, preen, and refine this false self partly in response to our childhood experiences, partly in response to the fallen society around us, and partly in response to sinful impulses within us. Various childhood experiences might shape our false self. Maybe at age eight we lost a close friend when our family moved to a new town, and that loss made us sad and lonely. Possibly our siblings were vastly different from us, with different personalities, interests, and ways of seeing the world, making us feel out of place in our own family.

Our false self also develops as society entices us to conform. We are pressured to buy until we are hopelessly in debt. We're pushed to have the newest computer, the fastest motorcycle, the biggest sport utility vehicle, the fanciest house. We are urged to excel, compete, and succeed in order to become the best, the smartest, the most powerful. As we participate in these urgent demands, our false self takes shape.

Another stimulus for the false self is our inherent egocentricity. We are inclined to pamper ourselves, perhaps, or to pursue our own interests above those of everyone else. We might, for example, envy the accomplishments and acquisitions of another person, wishing we had them for ourselves. Or perhaps we slip into gluttony, which is not simply about eating too much food, but more generally is about overconsuming any resource to such an extent that others are forced to get by with a much smaller, and perhaps inadequate, amount. Selfish inclinations have a way of feeding themselves so that the more we satisfy them, the more we want them. We live for our own self rather than living for neighborliness. As a result of these insidious traps, the false self feels wounded, angry, bitter, and afraid. It wants revenge. It tries to squash other people. It hates. From our false selves come the evils of war, racism, and terrorism.

Yet as we grow by degrees into the glory of God after our baptisms (see 2 Corinthians 3:18), our false self begins to diminish, while our true self slowly takes on more life. In response to grace and discipleship, the false self begins to die—sometimes painfully. It gets nailed to the cross and gradually withers, allowing our true self to emerge gradually into God's purifying light. As our transformation into God's glory expands, we then begin to grow the fruit of the Spirit (see Galatians 5:22-23).[12]

The Dark Night as Death of the False Self

The dark night helps the false self to wither. It's not the only way the false self can dry up, but it is one way. Although few Christians talk about the dark night, it commonly happens to many of us as a normal part of our discipleship. At its most intense, a dark night can make us feel, as Jesus felt on the cross, that God has abandoned us, although in fact God never leaves us. Despite the way we may feel, the dark night is actually one of God's tools for freeing us from the sin in our false self. It liberates our true self. God heals us during the night, and through an expression of divine light and love, helps our true self to flourish. The false self will continue to remain with many of us in some form for most, perhaps all, of our lives. But thanks to God's grace working in us, the false self's influence on us will be much reduced.

Our salvation lies in accepting God's grace and following Jesus daily. As the false self shrinks, God gradually purifies us of the evils and sins to which we are prone, shaping us after the pattern of Christ. Our true self becomes more intimate with God and aligned with God's purposes for the world (see John 15:1-8). We become Christ's arms and hands, his legs and feet, living new life for others. Call it embracing the cross.

Part 2

THE NIGHT'S ROLE

—3—

LEARNING TO KNOW GOD

I will meditate on all your work,
and muse on your mighty deeds.
—Psalm 77:12

How does the dark night begin, develop, and conclude? The answer varies from person to person. But to illustrate one way the dark night may unfold, we trace the story of a young woman named Laura as she experiences the first flush of enthusiasm for following Christ, the onset of a dark night, and the emergence into the dawn of contemplation. Her story will continue through chapter 6.

Falling in Love

One weekend near the end of her junior year in high school, Laura drove to a neighboring state to visit a cousin. That Saturday night, the two young women went to a youth rally where several bands performed contemporary Christian music. It was Laura's first full-throttle exposure to this music, and she immediately fell in love with the driving rhythms and raw power that swept her up into the presence of God.

Laura had grown up a congregation that sang traditional hymns. Her parents, strong supporters of classical music, saturated Laura and her siblings with composers such as Bach, Beethoven, and Brahms. In the second grade she started piano lessons. By age fourteen, she was playing the piano prelude and offertory once a month in worship.

Laura came home from the weekend with her cousin converted to contemporary Christian music. Although she knew it would vex her parents, she downloaded MP3 files of songs by the bands she had heard at the youth rally and listened to them for hours in her room with the volume cranked. She talked excitedly about her new love to friends at school, trying to get them interested in the same music. At church she buttonholed worship committee members and fellow musicians about starting a praise band that could play in church.

Seeing an opportunity, Laura's pastor called her one evening to invite her to attend a class at church to explore baptism. With gusto Laura consented, quickly deciding she wanted to commit herself publicly to following Jesus. She perceived how sin had wormed its way into her life—how catty she could be with her friends at school, how stuck up she could act while hanging around people who received lower grades than she did, how repulsed she felt when her parents dragged her along to help at the local homeless shelter and she had to play with seven-year-olds she did not like. Recognizing her need for redemption, Laura decided to welcome Jesus' cleansing power into her life.

Honeymoon

Baptism and its immediate aftermath were all Laura had hoped for. On the Sunday of her baptism, it seemed Jesus was palpably present, delighting her, renewing her, laughing with her. The awareness of Jesus motivated her to read the Bible for fifteen minutes every night, meditate on what she read, and pray for her friends and acquaintances. This was so sweet that she decided to study and pray even more. To the fifteen minutes before bedtime, she added another fifteen minutes of Bible study after school, occasionally jotting down insights that came to her. Then she prayed out loud, praising the wonderful name of Jesus.

Laura talked excitedly about the wonders of Jesus and the delights of contemporary Christian music to anyone she thought would listen. "You should be baptized too," she urged acquaintances at school, "because Jesus will like totally change your life as he has mine. And if you need help, I have some awesome music to recommend to you."

Laura also responded to Christ's work in her by engaging in acts of service to others. When the summer Bible school coordinator at church asked for volunteers, Laura eagerly signed up to bake all the cookies for Tuesday evening's snack. When her family went back to help again at the homeless shelter, she acted more willing than she had in years and tried hard to love the children she did not find very lovable.

Laura thought her spiritual life was great, except for Sundays, when she grew exasperated with the adults in her congregation who didn't act as excited about Jesus as she thought they should and who persisted in singing those stodgy hymns. "Yes," she emailed her best friend one afternoon, "I feel like I've really got Christianity down— I know how to follow Jesus, serve the Lord, and let the Spirit lead me. Jesus is so close and vibrant. This is great!" Laura confidently expected that her walk with Jesus was going to be like this for the rest of her life.

Early Enthusiasm

Attracted to Jesus by a different kind of music than she had grown up with, Laura had fallen in love with Christ. An early enthusiasm for God is common, though not universal, among new Christians. At some point in the life of faith, perhaps earlier, perhaps later, Christians often fall in love with something related to faith. The objects of our love could be a particular religious ideal (such as a seamless pro-life stance), a certain theology (such as liberation theology), a distinctive style of worship (such as charismatic praise), a riveting religious leader (such as a famous preacher), a certain community of people (such as a local congregation), or a special type of prayer (such as intercession). In the first flush of spiritual excitement we eagerly invest ourselves in this object of our love. We experience something of a honeymoon. This is a normal movement in the Christian life that we typically find spiritually rewarding.

Human lovers in the first flush of passion act similarly. They spend as many moments together as they can. They eagerly look each other in the face, hold hands, and sit on the sofa with their arms around each other. They take long, private walks. They talk for hours about their likes and dislikes, their hopes and dreams, their family and friends, what's important to them and what's not so important to them. The relationship gives them significant emotional rewards. Their attraction to each other and their excitement over new possibilities propels lovers into a deeper relationship.

People in love not only talk a lot with each other, but in the rare moments when they're not together, they also talk about their beloved to others. One year in college I roomed with a friend who had fallen in love with a woman on campus. Whenever he wasn't with her, he sat around in our dorm room endlessly reporting to me all the exciting things she said and did, describing how cute her nose was, and telling how fine she looked as she walked down the sidewalk. One day I could stand it no more. "Mike," I said, "give it a rest! In a dozen different ways you've already told me how wonderful she is. You don't need to keep telling me. I believe you."

Laura displays some of my roommate's behaviors. Her ability to speak is more developed than her ability to listen. She talks a lot *to* Jesus, building her prayers on a torrent of words; and she talks a lot *about* Jesus, using her enthusiasm to try to draw others into the same kind of relationship with God that she has. Not every Christian will fall madly in love with God as Laura did, but this intense, early enthusiasm about some religious ideal, theology, worship style, person, group, or practice does commonly happen to a greater or lesser degree.

Meditation

So far, Laura's religious life is oriented around spiritual practices that we can loosely group under the broad category of meditation. *Meditation* refers to spiritual activity that mainly involves our minds in a rational way, usually through words, ideas, or images. Meditation includes a broad array of faith practices, such as speaking, reading, writing, singing, teaching, preaching, memorizing—anything that mainly employs words and reason. The practices of meditation happen largely at our initiative; we decide what, when, and how to carry out these practices.

For example, the Sunday worship services at Laura's church mostly use varieties of meditation, all organized rationally around a particular theme, such as forgiveness, compassion for the poor, or keeping the Sabbath. The call to worship introduces the theme of the morning. The words of the songs pick up that theme in other ways. The children's story adds another dimension. The sermon expounds the theme in detail through biblical exegesis, story-telling, and concrete illustrations. The pastoral prayer gathers up thanksgivings, intercessions, and petitions, speaking them out loud into the ear of God. The benediction finally brings the theme to resolution. During the service, Laura and other worshippers play with this theme in their minds, comparing their own practices of forgiveness, compassion, or Sabbath with what they hear in the service, and imagining how they might live those practices more faithfully.

Much of North American Christianity organizes itself around

meditation, and not only in worship. Christian education classes normally use meditation as well, whether for children, youth, or adults. In a class for young children on the love of God, the teacher might have the students repeat the Bible memory verse out loud several times: "I trust in the steadfast love of God forever and ever" (Psalm 52:8).

Next the teacher might ask the students if they've ever been out in a boat on a lake when a storm came up. He might read aloud the story of Jesus stilling a storm on the sea when the disciples were afraid (see Mark 4:35-41). Finally the teacher provides games, puzzles, or other activities that help children understand that we can trust in God's steadfast love. All these activities are expressions of meditation. Using words, images, stories, and activities, the teacher slowly builds in children the knowledge of God.

Adult classes are usually varieties of meditation as well. If the class is a Bible study, the teacher provides information about the historical, cultural, and literary context of a passage. Class members then focus on analyzing the passage's content before discussing how it applies to their lives. In a sermon response class, the facilitator asks questions that nudge members to reframe the sermon's content, apply it to a slightly different context than the preacher did, or expand on the core message. Adult classes like these are led by human beings who employ discussion to instill in others the faithful habits of thought, feeling, and practice.

Laura and most of the rest of us grew up in this kind of church. Meditation is a normal and necessary part of Christian nurture. The practices of meditation have tremendous power to teach us the ways of God as revealed in Christ. Meditation steadily shapes our Christian character, rooting us in belief and doctrine, and molding patterns of holiness in us. The church appropriately pours a lot of energy into meditation because we have much to learn about God.

For most of us, the adventure of learning more about God

through meditation lasts a lifetime. During the first eighteen years of my life, I learned basic information about God in Sunday school. But as valuable as that beginning was, I soon discovered that what I learned in Sunday school was not enough. So over the next nineteen years, I set aside eight years of my life to receive formal education in Bible, theology, ethics, and Christian spiritual development. In addition to formal classroom education, I've been preaching and teaching the Bible almost every Sunday for over twenty years. Each year for the last ten years I've read ten to forty books about the Bible, theology, or church history.

I say none of this to brag, but to point out how little I still know about the ways of God, even after all that study. I've never studied carefully, taught, or preached extensively from Leviticus, Numbers, and Deuteronomy; Joshua and Judges; 1 and 2 Chronicles; Proverbs; most of Isaiah and Ezekiel; the bulk of the minor prophets; Ephesians and Colossians; and everything between 1 Timothy and Jude, with the exception of Philemon. I know relatively little about these sections of Scripture. Since I was eighteen, I've managed to study seriously only one-third to one-half of the Bible as measured by pages. I still have half to two-thirds of the Bible to go.

Getting to know God is a lifelong adventure that includes but also ranges beyond study. To the day of our death, we keep learning more about what God likes and dislikes, what priorities God has, what God values and disvalues, what God loves and hates, what is consistent with God' purposes and what is not. The more we know about God, the better we can hear God's voice and distinguish God's call on our lives. As a new Christian, Laura has only begun to explore the pathway of meditation. Later in life she will learn to use her mind to meditate on God in new ways (see Psalms 19:14; 49:3; 104:34; 119:97, 99).

Meditation has many expressions beyond the corporate life of the church. Imagine, for example, that you're alone in the car, driving somewhere, and you start thinking about a short passage from the Bible, such as Matthew 5:5: "Blessed are the meek, for they will inherit the earth."

You begin to wonder about that word *meek*. You reflect: "Who in my life has recently done something to illustrate meek? When was the last time I was meek, and how did that affect me and the people around me? What does meekness feel like from the inside? What helps me to be meek?" Then maybe you shift your thoughts to the public realm. You muse: "What would meekness look like in the mayor of my city? Has a president of the United States or a prime minister of Canada ever been meek? If so, how did he express meekness?" All these reflections may sound like daydreaming, but they're really a form of meditation. In meditation we let the truths of God take root in our heart and mind.

Another example of meditation is reading a Christian book. As you read, the author engages your intellect, will, and emotions around a certain topic. The Spirit then uses that book to shape your spiritual life. Consider one of the best-known books written by a Mennonite in the English language, the *More-with-Less Cookbook* (Herald Press, first published in 1976). That cookbook has influenced the way many Christians think about food. Using the simple strategy of printing beside the recipes vignettes of how people around the world treat food, Doris Janzen Longacre helped hundreds of thousands of people to consider how our commitment to Christ affects the way we eat and how the way we eat affects our commitment to Christ. Doris transformed the ordinary work of cooking into a spiritual practice. Her book taught us cooks how to meditate while we work in the kitchen. She showed us how to pray at the stove.

Some years ago I was in a small group that practiced another form of meditation. Each time we met, someone selected a brief Bible passage for us to concentrate on, usually a passage only a paragraph long. Then for an hour we sat together in silence, meditating on that passage using a process called *lectio divina*. I cannot speak for others in that group, but I noticed that by the end of the hour that portion of Scripture had become a part of me. The Spirit had planted it in my soul, and to this day, the passages we meditated on together have a special place in my life. Meditation plays a significant role in helping us learn about the God we worship and serve.

Contemplation

Though vital to the life of faith, the pathway of meditation offers us only a certain kind of knowledge about God. During our lifetime we may also develop another pathway of communication with God called contemplation, which differs from meditation in significant ways. Whereas meditation largely happens at our initiative, contemplation largely happens at God's initiative, although we can certainly open ourselves to God's gift of contemplation. Meditation uses words and images to help us learn more about God, while in contemplation we typically receive the transforming presence of God through love. In meditation we use our mind to analyze and understand, but in contemplation we focus our attention on God, which can include gazing at God with our inner eye. Meditation leads to knowledge about God; contemplation leads to a more intense awareness of God's love, light, and life.[13] Chapter 5 will explore contemplation in greater detail.

In many people, a dark night begins the path to contemplation and makes contemplation happen more easily. While it is not necessary to pass through a dark night to receive God's gift of contemplation, the dark night is in fact the doorway to contemplation (or perhaps to a deeper level of contemplation) for quite a few people. Laura was one of these. We continue with her story in the next chapter—the story of her dark night.

—4—

FEELING ABANDONED

O Lord, why do you cast me off?
Why do you hide your face from me?
—Psalm 88:14

In the last chapter, a newly baptized Laura fell in love with her Lord. Feeling enthusiastic, she energetically pursued evangelism and getting to know God better through the practices of meditation. She thought her relationship would remain on a spiritual high for the rest of her life, unlike other Christians who seemed to her to have a spiritless relationship with Jesus.

But her relationship with God did not remain on this spiritual high.

A Dark Night Begins

Seven months after her baptism, Laura noticed the excitement starting to evaporate. The contemporary Christian music she had downloaded from the internet no longer made her want to dance as it did at first. Thinking she probably just needed new music, she downloaded more MP3 files. For a few weeks these new songs stoked her inner fire, but then they too burned out. The music began to seem cloying and the lyrics simplistic. The driving rhythms of the drums irritated her so much that she turned her player off in frustration. "I wanted to cry because Jesus just wasn't there anymore. It didn't matter what music I listened to; I couldn't stand to hear it. I even went to the piano and tried playing some of my favorite classical music from childhood, but that didn't give me joy either."

The eagerness to convert other people to Jesus and contemporary Christian music fled her. "If I'm not full of Jesus," she reasoned, "then how can I persuade my non-Christian acquaintances to accept Christ? How can I be a vibrant witness when I'm not enthusiastic about Jesus anymore?"

Acts of service became downright distasteful. When the fellowship committee at church asked for volunteers to bake cookies for the annual Advent party, Laura did not feel like signing up, even though she did. When she finally dragged herself to the kitchen to mix the dough, she dashed the ingredients together, smashing bowls and baking sheets in anger at Jesus for leaving her. In January, when she went to the homeless shelter with her parents, her patience with the kids evaporated, and she had to step outside for a while to cool her anger.

By the end of her senior year in high school, Laura felt Christianity was hollow. One evening, something in her crumbled. As she tried to read the blessings and woes from Luke 6:20-26, the words had no life for her. Slamming her Bible shut and throwing it on the floor in disgust, she dropped to her knees and tried to pray for a friend at school who had just been diagnosed with lymphoma, but the words disappeared into space. "Jesus, where are you?!" she wailed, pounding her fists on the bed, "Why did you leave me?"

A dark night had entered Laura's life.

Disenchantment and Dryness

As the inability to connect with Jesus persisted, Laura felt frustrated and confused. Very little in her church experience had prepared her for this turn of events. She believed that a good, faithful Christian should always feel the presence of Jesus and live in a perpetual state of enthusiasm. Occasionally her pastors and Sunday school teachers had talked about spiritual dryness. But dryness, they implied, was the person's own fool fault. Dry Christians had a problem somewhere, they hinted, such as sin or laziness. Therefore the way to recover a living, growing relationship with Jesus was to try harder, fall on your knees, and repent before the throne of mercy.

"But I've just been baptized!" Laura told herself. "I confessed my sins and repented. I haven't committed some new sin, as far as I know. I fasted before my baptism. I've been regular in prayer and Bible study ever since. I've tried to witness and serve. So why this disconnect with Jesus? I don't understand!"

As often happens to people in the dark night, Laura did not know who to talk to about what was happening. No way would she talk to her parents, and she was afraid to admit what was really going on to any of her Christian friends. Her youth group leader or her pastor would listen sympathetically, she thought, but then in one way or another would probably just tell her to try harder. Maybe it would be better to put on an act and pretend that she and Jesus were still intimate. So she kept most of her true feelings to herself, only occasionally alluding to her best friend that "some things about Jesus I don't get." As the dryness continued, Laura allowed her practice of daily Bible reading and prayer to slip from once a day to several times a week. "What's the use?" she thought. "Jesus is not there anyway. Why should I bother?"

A Gift of God

During a dark night, it seems God has vanished, even though we continue to yearn for God. We can no longer pray with words or images, or at least we find it hard to do so. In general we feel spiritually dry. All three of these signs—the signs of a dark night—are happening to Laura. She is anguished about her inability to connect with Jesus. She cannot pray in the ways she formerly found meaningful. She finds no satisfaction in music, Scripture, or service.

Despite appearances, however, the dark night is actually one of the best things God does for us. A dark night is a profound expression of God's compassion because it strengthens our love for God over the long term. It deepens our faith in God, expands our friendship with God, and makes us more united to God's countercultural purposes in the world (more on this in chapters 11, 12, and 13). In the night, God helps us to become more spiritually whole. How does this happen?

Infatuation

To begin answering this question, recall that after Laura's initial conversion to Christian faith, her religious life had a certain amount of infatuation, similar to the infatuation two people express when they first fall in love. Caught up in the excitement of a new kind of music that gave her intense spiritual pleasure, Laura repeatedly turned to that music, expecting to receive a spiritual high each time she listened to it. For a while she did receive the high she wanted. God used this spiritual high to draw Laura closer, to keep her interested so that she and Christ could begin to form a genuine relationship with each other. In her early months as a Christian, the Holy Spirit poured a crucial foundation of love into the ground of her life.

But there was a problem. Laura was more in love with the music, and with the way the music made her feel, than she was with Jesus. She might have insisted that Jesus really was central in her life, and that music, Bible study, and prayer were secondary to that relationship. Perhaps Jesus truly was of primary importance to Laura in those early months after her baptism, but her dark night suggests that music, Bible study, and prayer were not quite as secondary as she might have thought. That she felt frustrated when music no longer gave her a spiritual fix shows she had become deeply attached to the music and to the emotion it stirred in her rather than to the God who was beyond the music. The act of throwing her Bible on the floor in exasperation suggests that she was measuring the effectiveness of Bible study by the way it made her feel. Laura was attached to her spiritual practices and to the pleasure she derived from them.

Attachment

One of the chief problems of human nature is our tendency to become attached to things that are not God. Most of us realize how easily we become attached to physical objects, such as the new car in our garage, the fabulous laptop we just bought, or the estimated worth of our shares in a mutual fund. With some reflection, we might also recognize that we could become attached to a person, such as a mentor who takes us under her or his tutelage to guide us through a particular phase of our life; to a new friend whom we want to be with at every waking moment; or to family, either to an ideal of what our family life should be or to specific members of our family, such as a spouse or a child. But few of us see that we can also become attached to "spiritual" things—to a particular pastor whose sermons we think are wonderful, to a church building that has unique architectural features that delight us, to the way our congregation fills the sanctuary with sound when we sing.

Laura became attached to a particular style of music and to the emotional rush it gave her. Others in her situation can, and often do, become attached to a certain method of Bible study, a specific practice of prayer, or a religious ideal such as "the baby killers have to be stopped" or "give justice to the poor." *Which* object, practice, feeling, or ideal we attach ourselves to is not the issue here (unless the thing itself is evil, in which case that is clearly a problem). The problem we are concerned with here is the attachment itself.

Attachments suck up our loyalty, keeping us from a full relationship with God. Attachments can, in fact, become our idols. From very early in our biblical faith, God knew we were going to have a problem with attachments and therefore warned us about them in direct terms: "You shall not make for yourself an idol, whether in the form of anything that is in heaven above, or that is on the earth beneath, or that is in the water under the earth. You shall not bow down to them or worship them; for I the LORD your God am a jealous God" (Exodus 20:4-5).

Yahweh, the God of heaven and earth, is a jealous God. I know a husband and wife who were talking one day about polygamy, the marriage practice in some traditional cultures where one husband has multiple wives. "Hon," the husband mischievously asked his wife, "how would you respond if you were only one of my three or four wives?" Her eyes flashing, the wife retorted, "Fine—as long as I'm the primary wife!"

Exodus 20:5 suggests that God feels the same way as this wife. When it comes to competition with our idols, God gets jealous. God wants to be the primary focus of our lives. God hopes for our deepest love and highest commitment, but our attachments to other things stand in the way. Our attachments relegate God to second or third or last place, and then God's original intention for intimacy with us cannot happen effectively. So in the dark night God dissolves our attachments to lesser things, including spiritual things, so that we are freer to love God as God.[14]

God's Mission

The dark night is a key part of God's missional purpose in the world. In biblical theology, God's mission mainly aims to create a new people of shalom and then to re-create those people when shalom falters. Originally God created the world to operate according to shalom (see Genesis 1–3). This well-being of creation was shattered when we humans succumbed to the sin of becoming attached to objects that are not God. These objects, symbolized by the fruit of the tree in the middle of the garden (see 3:3), looked alluring and beautiful. They promised to give us special knowledge and the power that comes from that knowledge. But as soon as we reached out for those things, held them greedily in our hands, and consumed them, those things disrupted our shalom with God (see 3:6). God was no longer primary. The pattern described in Genesis 3 of becoming attached to things less than God plays out repeatedly in our lives.

Our disobedience has had huge consequences. The consequence for us is that we have had to live with the reality of sin ever since. Sin dogs us in subtle ways we cannot always see until after the deed is done. We continue to become attracted to and ultimately attached to alluring things that promise much but give us little. We can become attached to almost anything that is not God: our possessions, our social standing, our self-image, our limited ideas about God. Becoming attached—holding tightly to our own equivalent of the fruit that is "a delight to the eyes" (Genesis 3:6)—usurps God's rightful place in our lives. We turn our possessions, social standing, self-image, spiritual practices, or human relationships into gods, and then the God of heaven and earth no longer has primacy of place.

Our Mission

God's key missional purpose is to create a world of shalom. We too have a missional purpose that bubbles up in response to God's mission of shalom. Someone once asked Jesus to name the central teaching of Scripture. He replied, "Hear, O Israel: the Lord our God, the Lord is one; you shall love the Lord your God with all your heart, and with all your soul, and with all your mind, and with all your strength" (Mark 12:29-30, quoting Deuteronomy 6:4-5).

To love God fully is the heart of our mission. Our love for

God leads to love for neighbor, to acts of service and witness, and to a sense of what our personal vocation in life is, even though we may change jobs numerous times. However, our love for wrong attachments takes up spiritual space that we could otherwise dedicate to loving God and others. Therefore, by helping to loosen our wrongful attachments, the dark night frees spiritual space in us to love God as God wants to be loved.

The Power of Attachments

Most of us cannot sever attachments using our own willpower. I certainly cannot. During the thirty-seven years since my baptism, I have often tried to break some of my sinful attachments, but again and again I have failed. I know Paul's lament only too well: "For I do not do the good I want, but the evil I do not want is what I do. . . . For I delight in the law of God in my inmost self, but I see in my members another law at war with the law of my mind, making me captive to the law of sin that dwells in my members" (Romans 7:19, 22-23).

Most of us are like this. With all our heart we want to break our attachment to go shopping when we feel bored, yet thirty minutes later we get in the car and head to the mall. We know that watching a particular television series harms our spiritual health, so we resolve to quit, yet five minutes before the show starts our willpower vanishes, and we turn on the television. We try hard to love someone we despise, yet our disgust rises unbidden when we think about that person, and so our efforts to love collapse. Our attachments control us so tightly that we cannot free ourselves. Much of our sin lies in becoming attached to what is not God and then worshipping the object of our attachment, whether a person, a possession, a feeling, or an ideal.

Since we cannot save ourselves from these attachments, we have little choice but to rely on God to do it. The consequence of our sin for God, therefore, is that God now has to work hard to free us. To regain first place in our lives, God must break these attachments to the lesser gods we have come to worship. God begins to do this when we turn to Christ, confess our sin, and accept baptism; but baptism is only the beginning of our conversion, not the end. Since we often commit serious sin and stumble into attachments after baptism, God has much re-creative work to do in us throughout our life of faith. Our continuing sin requires God to keep re-creating shalom by putting our relationships in proper order.

The dark night is an opportunity for God to re-create shalom after our baptism. It's one of God's tools—but not the only one—for drying up our attachments, reallocating our priorities, purifying our love, and refocusing our eyes not on the things that "delight" but on Christ, the founder and finisher of our faith (see Hebrews 12:1-2). During the dark night, our loss of satisfaction in things that once gave us pleasure comes precisely from the softening of attachments that God is causing within us. By reducing the pleasure we first felt when we bought our Toyota Prius, God is dethroning that god. By drying up the delight that rushed through us when we received a hefty pay raise, God discourages us from idolizing our income and the material possessions we can buy with it. By withholding from us the satisfaction we once found in a particular spiritual practice, God turns us away from worshipping the practice and refocuses our worship on God alone.

Spiritual Fasting

The dark night is a form of spiritual fasting. In physical fasting, we stop eating food for a time to focus ourselves more completely on God. Physical fasting can strengthen our relationship with God, as long as we have no medical issues that would cause fasting to harm our bodily health. The dark night accomplishes something similar, except that we fast from our attachments instead of fasting from sautéed chicken, rice and beans, or ice cream.

The spiritual fast of the dark night differs from a physical fast in several additional ways. First, physical fasts are relatively short, lasting for a meal, for three days, maybe even for forty days. Dark nights can be much longer. Many of them barely get underway in forty days, and may stretch on from months to decades. Second, in a physical fast we have considerable control over whether, when, and how to conduct the fast; but in a dark night, God decisively controls these things (although we do have a little influence). Third, when a physical fast is over, we normally go back to eating the full range of our normal diet. But when a dark night is over, we rarely go back to the attachment or attachments God dissolved.

For many years I was attached to television. I used to watch situation comedies, science-fiction adventures, Cubs baseball, and violent movies (odd for a pacifist, but true). Except for the violent movies, most of what I watched would probably be considered morally neutral. Nevertheless, I was attached to watching television, and the love inherent in that attachment kept me from giving some of my love to God and to others around me. At the time I did not recognize the harmful effect television was having on my relationships.

Then God led me into a dark night. I no longer had a visceral sense of the divine presence. As far as I could tell, I was not doing anything differently than I had always done. I did not detect any new sin in my life (although plenty of old sin still stuck to me). I had not slacked off in any of my spiritual practices, such as Bible study, prayer, worship, or service. Yet now all those spiritual practices went flat. It felt as if God, who once had seemed close enough for me to touch, deliberately walked away to see how I would respond.

I responded by desperately wishing God would come back. I believed God was still around me and still cared about me, but I could not understand why this wide distance now separated us. The distance fired my passion for God, just as my passion for my wife burns hotter when she and I are parted for one or two weeks. As the dark night continued, I noticed that, while my yearning for

God grew, my attachment to some other things withered. The attachment to television was one of several that dried up and died. *Star Trek*, Cubs baseball, and the nightly news no longer held much interest. So what if the crew of the starship Enterprise overcame all obstacles by the end of the show? They always did. So what if the Cubs lost today? That happens regularly. So what if the president retreated for a few days to Camp David for talks with the prime minister of some country? Presidents have been doing that for decades.

What I wanted more than anything else was to recover some sense of connection with God. In comparison with this great thirst for God (see Psalm 42:2), nearly everything else became less important. So thoroughly had God weaned me off television that in the spring of 2002 I completely stopped watching. I did not exactly make a conscious decision to quit; I just lost interest. I was more focused on God than I had ever been, and I knew I was not going to recover an intimate connection with God by watching *C.S.I.* or the *ABC Evening News*. Television looked vapid in comparison to God.

Only after the dark night had gone on for some years was I able to see that my love for television had been stealing my love for God. Once God softened my attachment to television, I was able to relinquish it, a lesser love, in order to offer more of myself to the great Lover of humanity. Since then I have had no interest in television, and during the rare moments when I watch a little at someone else's house or in a motel room, I am appalled by its banality. My attachment to television was decisively broken during this dark night. I confess I still have lots of other attachments, but at least that one is gone.

Purifying

Although we call it a *dark* night and although it can appear to be as deep as midnight, the night is never actually without light. Whether or not we perceive it—and often we cannot, particularly in the early stages of a dark night—God's flame is burning within us from the very moment the night begins. This divine flame slowly and secretly purifies us, as the fire of a metallurgist burns off impurities from precious metals. "For [God] is like a refiner's fire . . . he will sit as a refiner and purifier of silver, and he will purify the descendants of Levi and refine them like gold and silver, until they present offerings to the LORD in righteousness" (Malachi 3:2-3).

God's flame sparks the beginning of the dark night. Yet what we perceive as darkness does not really come from God, since God is light (see 1 John 1:5). The darkness we experience in the night comes instead from our sin and our stubborn reluctance to relinquish our attachments. Our experience of darkness and the painful detaching that goes along with it come from the purification God is achieving in our lives. For this reason, the metaphorical phrase *dark night* refers more to our subjective human experience of this process than to the objective work God is doing. It seems, feels, and looks to us like darkness, but actually God is extremely close to us, purifying the dross of our attachments and transforming us in love for love. God is burning off impurities so that our gold will become more pure.

Sometimes God's process of purification is relatively painless. Being detached from television was not very painful to me. But God's decision to wither another attachment brought me considerably more pain.

All my adult life, I have been attached to getting recognition from other people. When I became a pastor, I brought that attachment to recognition along with me into my work. As a pastor, of course I wanted to serve Christ and the church, but getting recognition from others gradually crept into my work and became my biggest motivator. Did I still want to preach and teach Scripture faithfully, to walk with people in crises, and to promote spiritual and missional growth? Of course. Did I still want to be faithful to God? Yes. Even so, what I really lived for was recognition and praise.

For the first seventeen years of ministry, I did not see my attachment. I thought my motives were pure. But they weren't pure—and only in the middle of a painful dark night that by then had lasted five years was I able to see my true motives. The god of recognition had snookered me, leaving me hollow, dry, and empty. I was snarfing up the junk food of praise and success but starving my soul. No one else was at fault; other people were just trying to affirm me. I was at fault for becoming attached to recognition instead of to God. The hollowness, dryness, and emptiness were signs that my motivation was twisted. At the time, I did not think so, but now I know that this pursuit of praise was subtly sabotaging my pastoral work. My spirit was increasingly corrupted. I was moving further away from purity.

This kind of thing happens often to good Christian folks. Perverse motivations sneak in, co-opt us, and hijack what we want to do for God. While pretending to serve others in the name of Christ, we scramble for prestige, struggle for control, compete for people and dollars, seek praise, pursue the illusion that big is automatically better than small, scheme for influence, and focus on appearance rather than substance. These occupational hazards of Christians happen in congregations, conferences, and denominations; in evangelism and social service ministries; in pastors and laypeople.

You might think that the solution is to examine our motives and then to dump the evil ones and keep the good ones. Maybe that helps sometimes. But for two reasons I doubt it's enough. First, often we cannot see our real motives. For seventeen years I could not see how caught up I was in getting praise from other people. Thanks to a dark night, only in retrospect do I understand better what was really happening to me. At this very moment I could easily be caught up in nefarious motivations that I cannot perceive, yet they are causing me to stumble on the path of discipleship. Second, even when we see our real motives, we cannot free ourselves from them. Steel ropes tie us fast, and no cutter or blowtorch lies within our reach. Sometimes changing is beyond our ability; sometimes our only hope is that God will liberate us.

God's Mercy

> Create in me a clean heart, O God,
> and put a new and right spirit within me. (Psalm 51:10)

Psalm 51 responds to this problem with prayer for a clean heart, for the gift of a new and right spirit. We pray for this because only God sees our true motivations and can finally make our heart clean. At baptism God's presence and power move in, permanently settling down to work on us. God opens the windows to air things out, sweeps up the dirt, repairs the plumbing, upgrades the electricity, lays down a new floor, paints the walls, runs a dust cloth over the woodwork, washes the soiled laundry, fixes the broken furniture, hangs up new pictures, and overhauls the landscaping. At baptism, God starts to build a home in us.

Once God moves in, true prayer is mainly about consenting to God's cleaning and constructing. Since God still has a lot of work to do on us after our baptism, prayer, at the most basic level, is about saying yes to God's renovations. In the dark night we will not always know what God is up to, because some of God's work happens beyond our perception. We will not always feel God's presence or recognize God's activity. Because some of what God does will be obscure to us, our role is to consent to the person, power, and presence of God. Consent is the basic attitude of prayer, whether we pray with words or in silence, whether we pray in a group or alone, whether we pray while moving around or sitting perfectly still. Saying yes to God, even when we aren't entirely sure what we're saying yes to, opens us to more of God's purifying love.

Some dark nights last only a few months, while others stretch out for decades. They can be mild or intense. We can go

Graduation:

Lee Roy, Joe, Anne, Malinda,
Beth

through more than one dark night in the course of our life (I have been through four so far). Whatever the length, intensity, or frequency of the night, our feelings of abandonment do eventually end. The night starts to shift. To see how that happens, we return to Laura's story.

—5—

RECEIVING GOD

We also boast in our sufferings, knowing that suffering produces endurance, and endurance produces character, and character produces hope, and hope does not disappoint us, because God's love has been poured into our hearts through the Holy Spirit that has been given to us.

—Romans 5:3-5

In the previous chapter we saw how the dark night removed most of the delight Laura felt in prayer, worship, Bible study, and service. God removed many of those delights to soften her unhealthy attachments and to help her become more passionate about God alone. Yet as the night continued, something new began to grow in Laura—a new way to pray.

Prayer in a New Mode

After graduating from high school and settling into summer vacation, Laura started to visit the city park near her house. At first, going to the park was just something to do on cool summer evenings, but the more she went, the more she wanted to keep going back. Her favorite spot to sit was on a picnic table at a bend in the river, where she could watch and listen to the water gurgling over the rocks. Without thinking of anything in particular or trying to accomplish a specific goal, she simply watched the bubbling water. This quiet place oddly contained the presence of Jesus in ways she couldn't articulate. Sitting by the river was not at all like being at her church's worship services, oriented as they were around a constant stream of words. Yet she came home from each visit to the park more settled, refreshed, and peaceful. As if some inner voice urged her, she continued going to the river about once a week.

When Laura started college in late August, most of her energies were invested during the early weeks in adjusting to a new environment and a new schedule. By October she began to get restless, as if something crucial was missing from her week. Several days later she realized what it was: she missed those weekly visits to the river in the park. "But where can I find a place like that around here?" she wondered. "I don't have a car, so I'm pretty much stuck on campus, and there's no river here."

On Tuesday morning of the following week, while walking to the library, Laura took a detour to explore parts of the campus she hadn't visited yet. There she found a secluded alcove surrounded by evergreen trees, and in the alcove, several stone benches. She laid her backpack down and chose the bench overlooking hills to the east. As she sat and breathed deeply from the crisp air, she felt more peaceful than she had since college began. "This is the place," she whispered to herself. "I'm coming back here as often as I can."

Which she did. For the rest of the school year Laura stopped by the alcove once, sometimes twice, a week. The autumn's variegated colors and falling leaves expressed the dying that she felt inside. When autumn became winter, the landscape of brown, matted grass and gray trees punctuated her sense of desolation. In the spring, the greening leaves seemed to call forth her yearning for God, for something new to arise within her. During that first year of college, the cycle of seasons suited her moods well.

Laura also turned more often to Scripture, not to her old favorites like the final five praise psalms (146–150) or the opening section of Ephesians, which waxes eloquent about the spiritual blessings we have in Christ (1:3-14), but to new passages that never caught her attention before, such as Psalm 63:1:

> O God, you are my God, I seek you,
> my soul thirsts for you;
> my flesh faints for you,
> as in a dry and weary land where there is no water.

That described pretty well what she felt she had been going through: wandering around in a desert, with Jesus far off in the distance and she in weary pursuit, fainting for communion with him. Glancing across the page of her Bible, she saw the opening line of the previous psalm, which made her think those quiet times by the river and out in the alcove had some biblical justification: "For God alone my soul waits in silence" (Psalm 62:1).

Waiting silently. That named what she had been doing for most of the year: waiting for Jesus, waiting to be filled with something new.

During spring break, Laura went home for a week. While she was there, her family's turn at the homeless shelter came around again. Now that she was in college and more on her own, she didn't feel compelled to go along, but she went anyway—with some trepidation, fearing that the evening would not go well and she might overreact to the kids. They were indeed their usual bouncy selves.

But while riding back home in the car afterward, Laura mused about her internal reactions that night as she had played with the children. Unlike previous times at the shelter, she had been relatively patient. When three-year-old Michael threw his dinner plate at the wall, she calmly cleaned up the mess without getting angry, as she would have on previous occasions. When eight-year-old Natalie obstinately refused to play Mouse Trap with the other children, Laura gave her a little space, then a few minutes later sidled up to her and gently asked if she would like Laura to read her a story. In previous situations like the one with Natalie, Laura realized she would have written the little girl off and allowed her to stew in the corner by herself for the rest of the night. Instead Laura made another overture, and when Natalie nodded yes, she would like to hear a story, the two of them sat down and had a good time together. "What's happening to me?" Laura wondered. "Why was I so different tonight? Why was I so patient with those kids, even so kind to them?"

The Pathway of Contemplation

The difference Laura noticed in herself came about as a result of contemplation. Until then, most of Laura's religious practices had used the pathway of meditation, which relies mainly on words and images (see chapter 3). But meditation is not the only pathway of communication with God. Another pathway is *contemplation*—an inflow of light and love from God. While this inflow of God's light and love may piggyback on words or images, its origin lies beyond them. Unlike meditation, which we largely control by deciding when and how to pray, contemplation lies more in God's control. In contemplation the Spirit decides when and how to pray in us.

> Likewise the Spirit helps us in our weakness; for we do not know how to pray as we ought, but that very Spirit intercedes with sighs too deep for words. And God, who searches the heart, knows what is the mind of the Spirit, because the Spirit intercedes for the saints according to the will of God. (Romans 8:26-27)

When Paul wrote these words, he may not have been thinking of what we now call contemplation. Yet what he describes fits contemplation. During the dark night and the rise of contemplation, we are weak before God. We do not know exactly what we need or how to go about getting it. We do not even know how to pray in the right way, because the old, familiar forms of prayer no longer work well for us. Therefore the Spirit "groans" (the literal meaning of the Greek) for us beyond what words can express. These groans are not mumbo-jumbo that God cannot understand, but an exquisite form of communication that the members of the Trinity understand thoroughly. In contemplation, the Spirit flows into us and also intercedes for us.

God eagerly wants to give us the gift of contemplation. Although we can open ourselves to this divine flow of love, hope, peace, and joy, we cannot control when it begins, how long it lasts, or when it ends. Usually contemplation comes in relative silence while we are doing something simple, such as sitting, strolling, drawing, playing relaxing music, or gardening. We can encourage contemplation by practicing simple loving attention to God and to God's creation. Contemplation may last only a few minutes or even a few seconds. Sometimes it begins and ends before we realize it. Or we may recognize it and then in the next instant realize it has ended. Like the two disciples from Emmaus who recognized Jesus and then watched as "he vanished from their sight" (Luke 24:31-32), we may recognize that the inflow of contemplation has been given to us only to notice in the next instant that it has suddenly come to an end. If the infusion of God's love is intense, we may feel our hearts burning. If the infusion is less intense, we may simply feel more centered, whole, peaceful, and loved. Regardless of how intense contemplation is or how long it lasts, the effects remain with us for a long time.

As Laura watches the water quietly gurgle over the rocks in the park, and as she gazes silently out over the hills on the edge of campus, she experiences the early stirrings of contemplation.

It may appear to casual passersby that Laura is simply wasting time, or daydreaming, but that is not so. While she quietly sits in God's creation, simply watching and listening, the Spirit pours grace, love, and shalom into her. Laura does two things to receive this infusion of contemplation from God. First, she heeds the inner voice of love that urges her to find restful places such as the city park and the alcove on campus. Second, when she arrives at these restful places she lays aside her cares and worries, and opens herself to God. God then does the rest. The quiet peace she feels is one clue that contemplation is happening to her. The more important clue lies in the patience she shows to children at the homeless shelter. As the flow of God's subtle love begins to create a new pathway in her, Laura discovers that she can unexpectedly, almost miraculously, live love in a difficult situation that formerly vexed her. Contemplation is converting her to a new way of life—the life of God's unique love.

Making Room for the Spirit

Subtle and brief, contemplation changes us in profound ways over time. So significant are these changes that we might think of them as a kind of second conversion after our baptism. As the dark night proceeds, the Spirit empties us of our attachments to false gods. This emptying creates more space for the Spirit to pour God's love into our hearts (see Romans 5:3-5). The dark night, therefore, is an emptying that prepares us for the filling of God's love and shalom through contemplation. It creates an inner space where we can receive some of God's most delectable gifts in a new way.

Although at some level we consent to it, we do not control this process of contemplation. Just as we cannot control the flow of sunlight to the earth, so we cannot control the flow of God's love into our bodies. As the intensity of sunlight can vary a great deal, depending on the time of day and on what clouds are drifting through the atmosphere, so too the intensity of contemplation can vary a great deal, depending on what God wishes for us at that particular moment and on how willing we are to receive the inflow God sends to us.

Generally we are most receptive to contemplation when our surroundings are quiet, although silence is not required for contemplation to come to us. Nevertheless, people in whom God is birthing contemplation usually search for more quiet in their lives, so much so that a yearning for silence may signal that God is sending contemplation our way. This is true for both introverts and extraverts. After the onset of a dark night and the birth of contemplation, extraverts often discover a new need for silence that they rarely encountered before. In the search for silence, extraverts may also seek periods of solitude.

Many Christians experience contemplation without realizing it or calling it by that name. What we call daydreaming may sometimes really be contemplation. Many times I've sat on the oak rocking chair in our living room, staring out the window at the ravine on the west side of our house. I see the rocks that previous owners spread at the bottom of the ravine to prevent erosion. I see the two tulip poplars, now nearly thirty feet tall, that we planted the first summer we lived here. A little further away I see our neighbor's pale yellow house and white pine trees.

If you tiptoed into the room and glanced at me, you might think I was daydreaming. Often you would be right; that's all I'm doing. While I'm staring out the window dozens of thoughts might be flitting through my head: ideas for next Sunday's sermon, the eggs I need to write down on the grocery list, the clusters of poison ivy I need to eradicate at the edge of the ravine, the oil that needs changing in the car. Emotions might also careen through me: anger at this person, gratitude for that person, sadness about the persistent violence in many countries.

But at other times, contemplation is happening while I sit in that rocking chair. My eyes, though still open, no longer notice the rocks and trees, but simply look without seeing anything in particular. My flitting thoughts halt. For a second, maybe a little longer, I see nothing, think of nothing, and feel no emotion. I am simply in the presence of God, and during that brief period, God's quiet love flows into me, if God wishes. Contemplation is pure awareness of God, without distractions or diversions.

Some people open themselves to contemplation by watching a wood fire. I wonder if this might partly account for the popularity of fireplaces and wood stoves in homes, chimeneas on backyard decks, and wood fires at campgrounds. Perhaps it also helps to account for the popularity of candles in worship services and homes. Dancing flames seem to put many of us, even children, into a contemplative frame of mind, during which God may well be communicating with us in ripples of silence too deep for words.

Weaning

The dark night signals the growth of contemplation. Compare it to a parent weaning an infant. For the first months of life, the only food appropriate for an infant is breast milk or a substitute like formula. But since he or she cannot grow to full physical maturity on milk alone, parents soon try to interest the child in rice cereal, and a little later, in puréed peas and applesauce. The weaning process is simple: instead of offering milk, parents offer other food. At first the infant fights this. The child is used to milk, likes it very much, and sees no reason to swallow anything else. But parents know that for good physical and mental development, the child must learn to eat adult food, such as carrots and pears.

In the dark night, God weans us off the diet of meditation and interests us in the food of contemplation. Meditation is the normal, natural, and ideal food at the beginning of our Christian life, but contemplation is more useful for our long-term discipleship and spiritual maturity. Particularly at the beginning of the dark night, we feel abandoned because we are no longer receiving the milk we've come to enjoy. We yearn for the familiar patterns and satisfactions of meditation. In deep pain, we think God is playing some cruel trick on us. An infant who has been accustomed to milk reacts this way too. Nothing in the child's experience has prepared it to realize that cherry cobbler is also food. It might spit the cobbler out and refuse to eat it. But a parent will keep trying, just as God keeps trying to interest us in contemplation, even if we keep spitting it out.

We should not think that once God introduces us to contemplation, we never go back to meditation again. Infants grow into adults and eventually learn to eat everything from mangoes to filet mignon, yet most adults still consume milk or milk by-products throughout their lives. I'm well past middle age, and I've never quit eating milk, cheese, butter, sour cream, and ice cream, but they are only a portion of the hundreds of other foods I eat. Similarly, Christians to whom God gives the food of contemplation will continue to benefit from the practices of meditation. Not only are both pathways of prayer useful for a balanced diet, but in many spiritual practices we can easily alternate from meditation to contemplation and back to meditation again, all in the space of a few minutes. During the dark night we may not be able to use the pathway of meditation very much, but once contemplation has become a regular and constant part of our diet, the night ends, and most of us can enjoy some of the practices of meditation again. As God's contemplative love flows into us, the new diet enables increasing spiritual maturity. We are simultaneously freed from some of our attachments and filled with "a new and right spirit" (Psalm 51:10).

Contemplation in Personal Life

One of my dark nights lasted seven years. For the first five years, the intensity of the night was mild. I could still engage in some kinds of meditation, such as inductive Bible study and vocal prayer, although contemplation was clearly beginning to take root in my life as well. Then, late in the fifth year, the weaning of the night became intense. Virtually all types of meditation that I had been doing for the previous twenty-five years fell away. I simply could not make myself do intercessory prayer. Bible study of the kind I had learned in Sunday school, college, and seminary became almost impossible.

Most difficult of all were Sunday-morning worship services. For more than six months, sitting in worship was deeply frustrating. The worship planners weren't doing anything different; they still did the good job they had always done. Instead the dark night was changing my patterns of prayer. I could not sing anything, even my favorite songs. Focusing on what other people said in the worship service was so hard that most of the time I just gave up and didn't even try to listen. When the other pastor of our congregation preached, I tried my best to follow her words, but I could not. At best I could listen to someone for perhaps a minute, but after that I was unable to grasp what he or she was talking about. All the spoken parts of worship—the call to worship, children's stories, sermons, announcements, sharing of joys and concerns, pastoral prayers, and benedictions—were like a blast from a fire hydrant, spraying so many words at me I couldn't focus. Mercifully, I was still able to preach and lead pastoral prayers, although both were so difficult to do that at the time I sincerely wished I were not a pastor.

Two spiritual practices gave me peace. The first was looking at simple, beautiful objects. After I finished preaching during one particularly aggravating worship service, I sat down in the front row of chairs, desperate for an escape from the barrage of words. My eyes eventually rested on the banner behind the pulpit. The banner had no words (what a mercy!), only plain, abstract forms, and I discovered that by focusing on it I could let go of the ceaseless march of words in the rest of the worship service. Outside of worship services, I also found peace by gazing at naturally beautiful things from God's creation, such as leaves and flowers. So I spent a lot of my spare time just looking at things. I didn't try to analyze them or do anything with them. I only looked, and the looking was enough.

The other spiritual practice that gave me peace was silence. On Mondays when I had a day off, when Jenny was at work and our boys were in school, I silently sat alone in the house for most of the day. I did not listen to music or watch television. As much as possible, I refrained from starting the dishwasher, washing machine, or clothes dryer. Sometimes I also turned the telephone off. This deep silence, broken only by cars occasionally driving by, settled me into relative tranquility.

In all of this, God weaned me away from meditation to interest me in contemplation. As I gazed at simple objects and sat in blessed silence, God prayed in me with sighs and yearnings beyond words. When that dark night passed, I was able to reengage some forms of meditation, such as vocal prayer and analytical Bible study. The wordiness of worship does not bother me quite as much as it once did. I can listen carefully now when other people preach. I can sing again.

The dark night has made contemplative prayer a significant part of my discipleship. Contemplation refreshes me in ways that meditation does not. Contemplation is also reshaping areas of my life, particularly some of my attitudes and behaviors. For example, I used to get angry with other drivers for stupid things I thought they did on the road. That rarely happens anymore, and even when it does, my anger is generally less intense.

Contemplation in Church Life

Notwithstanding American church life being oriented around meditation, here and there you can see congregations opening themselves to God's gift of contemplation. An obvious example is the traditional silent meeting that some Quakers practice. Participants sit silently in loving attention to God to receive God's contemplation if and when God chooses to give it.

In most other denominations, music may be the closest the

worship services get to contemplation. Thanks to a recent sabbatical that my congregation generously gave me, I was able to visit other churches in my community. Some of the churches I visited had bands that led worship for the first half-hour from the stage at the front. Usually the band started off with rousing, upbeat praise songs and tried, with varying degrees of success, to get people in the congregation involved by clapping their hands and singing along. This first part of the service seemed to be a variety of meditation. Using their minds, people in the congregation followed the words projected on the screen, tried to get all the notes right, and clapped in rhythm. But later in the half-hour, the band often switched to quieter music that most people knew well. As the quieter song repeated itself, many band members and many in the congregation closed their eyes and appeared to enter a zone of prayer beyond meditation. Although I could not be certain, at this point in the service these people might have been opening themselves to contemplation.

Most of the congregations I've been a member of generally sing hymns rather than praise music. During my most recent dark night (the one that lasted seven years), I sometimes received brief gifts of contemplation as the congregation sang hymns. These moments came entirely without warning, lasted several seconds at most, and left me in tears of gratitude. It was as if the Spirit swooped in with the speed of an eagle, brushed my desolate spirit ever so lightly with wingtips of love, and swooped away as rapidly as it came. This happened only once every few months.

More than most Protestant worship services, Taizé-style worship bridges meditation and contemplation. Taizé services use Scripture readings and music that at first appear to fall into the category of meditation. But the way these services use Scripture and music is highly contemplative. The lack of sermons and announcements enhances the contemplative atmosphere, as does the practice in some places of lighting candles as an act of intercession for others, without using words.[15]

Certain types of prayer are highly compatible with contemplation. Centering prayer, which can be practiced both by individuals and by groups, is specifically designed to prepare us for receiving contemplation. After choosing a word that symbolizes your consent to God's action in you, you sit quietly in a comfortable position for twenty minutes with your eyes closed. When you notice yourself becoming caught up in a thought or an emotion, you gently return to the word that you chose when you began. At the end of twenty minutes, you remain in silence for a few minutes more before returning to your activities. Simple to learn, centering prayer has opened the door to God's contemplation for hundreds of thousands of people, especially when practiced twice a day.[16] Centering prayer may be the most effective way of welcoming contemplation.

Contemplative prayer is not limited to sitting still. We can also prepare ourselves to receive God's flow of love when our bodies are in motion. While walking or running, many people have found it meaningful to say the Jesus Prayer ("Lord Jesus Christ, Son of God, have mercy on me," sometimes with the addition of "a sinner" at the end of the sentence). They repeat this prayer over and over until it becomes so embedded in their lives that it essentially prays itself. Once the prayer takes on a life of its own, our hearts and minds can at moments move beyond the words to a different zone of awareness where contemplation flows.

For four years, I said the Jesus Prayer every afternoon when I came home from the office and exercised by walking through our neighborhood. While walking I slowly repeated the prayer, matching the syllables of the words to the pace of my stride. I no longer do the Jesus Prayer very often, preferring centering prayer instead, but during a recent illness the Jesus Prayer came back to me in a profound way. For about a week I was confined to bed with an excruciatingly painful illness. I quickly discovered that the only prayer I could manage was the Jesus Prayer because all others were beyond my ability. The Jesus Prayer was so embedded in my life that it became the fallback prayer when all others failed.

Walking a labyrinth is another way to open us to contemplation while in motion. I have friends, both women and men, for
whom this is their favorite way to pray. A labyrinth is a little like
the mazes many of us traced with our pencil when we were children, except there is only one path to follow, and no dead ends.
You start at the entrance and slowly wind your way around the
path until you come to the center. You pray in the center for a
while, and when you're done, you follow the path back out again.
Typically labyrinths are set up outside in the grass, although the
floors of churches are sometimes built with labyrinths laid out in
tile. I know a man who made a beautiful finger labyrinth for his
wife out of grooved wood, small enough to fit in one's lap.
Instead of walking in an outside labyrinth, with your fingers you
follow the groove in the wood to the center, pray, and then trace
your finger back out again.[17]

The arts can be a conduit of contemplation. Instrumentalists
may experience contemplation while playing their instrument,
particularly if they know the music well. Potters, painters, photog-
raphers, and other artists may slip into the sphere of contemplation while they work. The well-known twentieth-century contemplative Thomas Merton took photographs as a way to rehearse his
contemplative seeing.

Contemplation can happen while reading the Bible too. *Lectio
divina*, a form of Bible reading and prayer, arose early in the
church's history as a route to contemplation. Lectio divina has four
movements—reading a passage in the presence of God, ruminat-
ing on a particular word or phrase in the passage, responding to the
passage with spontaneous prayer (all three of these are basically
forms of meditation), and resting in God beyond thoughts or
action—which can lead to contemplation. These four movements
are like points around the circumference of a wheel. You can start
anywhere along the wheel and move to any other place on the
wheel as the Spirit leads you.

You can do lectio divina by yourself or in a group with other people. For a number of years I was in several small groups that did lectio every time we met. Although I no longer see the members of those groups very often, to this day each of them has a special place in my heart. Lectio not only opens us to contemplation, it also builds communion with God and with others in the group.[18]

Subtle Effects

Contemplation can be so subtle and hidden that we might not realize that God's healing love has just flowed into us. We can get up from the most frustrating experience of prayer or the driest session of Scripture reading, thinking to ourselves, "Well, that was a waste of time. Nothing happened." And yet God very well could have addressed us at some deep level of our soul that we know nothing about. God's ability to work in us does not depend on how we feel about things. Similarly, we can walk away from the most unrewarding act of service or the most boring worship service, wondering whether anything worthwhile happened. Maybe we're right that nothing significant happened—but then again, maybe something important did happen in us or in others that we could not see. Just because *we* think nothing good is happening in our spiritual practices does not mean we are spiritually dead.

Sometimes we make more progress toward the goal God has in mind for us when we feel spiritually dead than when we feel spiritually alive. The way our relationship with God feels is not a reliable thermometer of how hot or cold we actually are. God might accomplish far more important and wonderful things in us when we feel desolate than when we get up from prayer on fire for Christ, when we have a revolutionary insight into some Scripture passage, or when our spirits are going to burst with praise in worship.

How then can we tell whether contemplation is happening? Sometimes we can't, at least not yet. It often takes a while to realize that contemplation is working in our lives, especially in the early and middle portions of a dark night. In the latter parts of a dark night, contemplation is generally more noticeable. Even so, there are signs to look for. The surest signs are the growth within us of at least one fruit of the Spirit: love, joy, peace, patience, kindness, generosity, faithfulness, gentleness, or self-control (see Galatians 5:22-23). The fruit of the Spirit often grows slowly, just like fruit in nature. One of my friends grows apples in his back yard. Since the trees are between the house and the garage, he walks by them nearly every day in the spring and summer. "I never see much change from one day to the next," he says, "but I certainly do see change from one month to the next."

The growth of spiritual fruit is like that. We see growth over a long period but rarely over short periods. Sometimes the best way to find out if God is growing Spirit fruit in us is to ask someone who knows us well, such as a friend, a colleague at work, or our spouse. At other times we notice a difference in our own actions, as Laura did. The unusual patience that she had for children at the homeless shelter is a strong sign that the fruit of contemplation is growing. God's mission of creating shalom is taking effect in her.

Whenever and however it happens, contemplation is a wonderful gift that guides us into spiritual territory that meditation rarely visits. An acquaintance of mine calls contemplation "the cream" of our relationship with Christ. Ephesians describes it as this: "to know the love of Christ that surpasses knowledge, so that you may be filled with all the fullness of God" (3:19).

—6—

EMERGING INTO THE DAWN

[Jesus] cried out with a loud voice, "Lazarus, come out!"
—John 11:43

In the previous chapter we noticed how Laura experienced the beginning of contemplation—the peaceful, loving inflow of God—by the river near her home and in the secluded alcove on the college campus. On the way back from the homeless shelter, she realized that she had been unusually patient with the kids at the shelter and recognized it as a sign that the Spirit was birthing newness in her. Although she could not see it right away, Laura was beginning to emerge from her dark night into the dawn of God's new creation.

Precious and Honored

Through her freshman year of college, Laura visited the secluded alcove on campus once or twice a week, generally staying for about fifteen to twenty minutes each time. On Sunday mornings at church she sat quietly at the side of the sanctuary, some-times singing and other times not, sometimes listening to the wor-ship service and other times losing herself contemplatively in the light pouring into the windows, but rarely talking to others unless they spoke to her first.

One Sunday before the sermon, the worship leader stood behind the pulpit and read parts of a psalm Laura did not remem-ber hearing before.

> Where can I go from your spirit?
>> Or where can I flee from your presence? . . .
> If I say, "Surely the darkness shall cover me,
>> and the light around me become night,"
> even the darkness is not dark to you;
>> the night is as bright as the day. (Psalm 139:7, 11-12)

The words captivated her. She reached for the nearest pew Bible, opened it to Psalm 139, and soaked up the words "the darkness shall cover me." That image fit what she had been going through: a foggy season of life when she could not see ahead very well, where the scenery and the road signs were obscured. And yet "the darkness is not dark" to God, she noticed. "God in my darkness?" she mused to herself. "God sees through the darkness even if I can't?" But the words that really tugged her were "the night is as bright as the day." She let the phrase repeat itself in her over and over, as the pastor, whom she did not want to listen to today, droned his sermon. *The night is as bright as the day. The night is as bright as the day.*

That sentence floated in Laura for the rest of the week. Rather than analyzing the words, she let them soar and dart in inner space. "They gave me a lot of hope," she later remembered. "They stirred me, helped me to believe that God had to be nearby, lurking in the shadows of my life, if only my eyes could adjust to glimpse this God. Hearing those words that Sunday was a turning point."

Encouraged by this way of using the Bible in a prayerful

rather than an analytical, studious way, Laura tried it with other passages. One passage became particularly meaningful:

> But now thus says the LORD,
>   he who created you, O Jacob,
>   he who formed you, O Israel:
> Do not fear, for I have redeemed you;
>   I have called you by name, you are mine.
> When you pass through the waters, I will be with you;
>   and through the rivers, they shall not overwhelm you;
> when you walk through fire you shall not be burned,
>   and the flame shall not consume you.
> For I am the LORD your God,
>   the Holy One of Israel, your Savior. . . .
> You are precious in my sight,
>   and honored, and I love you. (Isaiah 43:1-4)

She started by inserting her own name in the fifth line so that it read, "I have called you by name, Laura, you are mine." This amended sentence hovered in her mind for weeks, making her feel less abandoned by God. Then her attention shifted to the last lines, "you are precious in my sight, and honored, and I love you." This similarly swirled around, making her feel cherished even as the obscure darkness continued to weigh heavily on her.

When her college classes concluded in May, Laura found a summer job working for a painting contractor. She liked the variety of painting both outside and indoors, sometimes bantering with the other members of the painting crew, but more often working in silence. After she got the hang of using scrapers, brushes, and rollers, she discovered that the light physical activity calmed her mind enough that on most days she entered, for a while, an internal zone of quiet centeredness that left her refreshed. It was sort of prayerful.

That summer she discovered she could occasionally listen to music again without getting frustrated, both the classical music of her childhood and the Christian rock of her senior year in high school. But her relationship to the music was different now. She no longer grabbed it tightly, but held it gently with open hands. She appreciated it as it was, for what it was, not for how it made her feel. She neither needed it nor relied on it. Music had changed from a crutch into a companion.

When classes started again in August, Laura ran into Kwajalene, a friend from the previous year whom she had not seen all summer. They decided to catch up over coffee. After they talked for about half an hour, Kwajalene leaned across the table and said, "You know, Laura, you seem more relaxed, more settled, than you were last year. You're not as moody. Something's changed. What happened to you over the summer?"

"God," replied Laura. "God and I are in a new place with each other. Maybe I'm more centered in God than I was before."

Emerging

Perhaps neither Laura nor Kwajalene would have used the word, but the change Kwajalene noticed in Laura was *emergence*. The biblical story of Lazarus coming out of the tomb symbolizes the emergence that happens in us toward the end of the dark night. The tomblike death of the dark night lasted about eighteen months for Laura, but in other people it might last for a different length of time. The length of our dark night depends partly on how long it takes God to accomplish the changes in us that God desires and partly on how willing we are to cooperate with God in this process.

Lazarus stayed in the darkness of the tomb for four days (see John 11:39). An interesting and sometimes overlooked detail of this story is that Jesus deliberately let Lazarus die. When Lazarus became ill, his sisters, Mary and Martha, sent a message from their home village of Bethany to Jesus, who was staying somewhere near the Jordan River (see 10:40). Their brief message made no demands but simply informed Jesus of the situation: "Lord, he whom you love is ill" (11:3). Instead of rapidly hiking right over to Bethany, about ten miles away, and rescuing Lazarus from his illness, Jesus lingered for two whole days. He had no particularly urgent business to attend to; he just dawdled. Only on the third day did he trek westward to Bethany. By then Lazarus had been dead four days. Jesus loved Lazarus, Mary, and Martha very much; but he deliberately let Lazarus die (see verse 5).

This story suggests that while Jesus could rescue us from the dark night, he does not. Instead he stands by in a location that seems distant from us, waiting for the night to do its work and run the course he wishes it to run. When we've been in the dark tomb long enough, Jesus "arrives" (he was never far away), and in some way calls us to "come out" (verse 43). That's when we start to emerge from the night.

Lazarus's emergence from the tomb did not happen in the twinkling of an eye. It took time. First the stone had to be rolled away (see verse 39). Meanwhile Jesus stood by, talking with Martha (verses 39-40). Next Jesus prayed (verses 41-42). Only then did he yell at Lazarus to emerge from the tomb. Yet Lazarus's emergence was still not complete. He stumbled out of the tomb readily enough, but he was still wrapped from foot to forehead in strips of burial cloth and had to wait while other people, at the command of Jesus, unwrapped him (verse 44)—a process that probably took at least several minutes, followed by more time for hugs, kisses, and laughter. Very likely all this was followed by some sort of celebration meal that took still more time to prepare and eat.

It takes time to emerge from a dark night. Don't expect it to happen in a few days or even a few weeks. The process of emerging may last months, possibly a few years, and even then we may not emerge into the brilliant light of a noonday sun. Often we find that when we emerge from a dark night, the light in front of us is more like a sunrise. Consider what happens in the gradual transition from night to sunrise. At first the fragile light of the new day is barely perceptible; at this stage we sometimes wonder if the sun is rising at all or if we're just seeing things. Gradually we see enough evidence—distinct tree bark, individual blades of grass—to say for sure that the sun is indeed coming up. Some minutes later, depending on atmospheric conditions, glorious hues slowly spread across the sky, and eventually the sun itself peeps over the horizon. Day is on the way.

Laura's dark night was relatively mild and typical of the kind many of us have. She thought her night was plenty intense, and in a sense it was. But some of us have had, or will have, even more intense dark nights than hers, if God wishes to purify our harmful attachments even more deeply. Generally the more intense God makes our night, the more intense will be the light God shows us as we emerge. Since Laura's night was more moderate than some, her emergence was proportionally subtle. Rather than having a sudden, hugely radical shift, her shift in spiritual practices, sensibilities, and behaviors was more subdued. Nevertheless Kwajalene noticed that she was more settled—a state of affairs that Laura accurately labeled as "more centered in God." Her experiences of prayer in church, with Scripture, and while working on the painting crew after her freshman year were all moving in a contemplative direction.

Our night doesn't always end in a steady, even trajectory. For a while we may see the growing dawn, and then, much to our frustration, we find ourselves thrust for a while back into the tomb of transformation with the door rolled shut again. God's purpose in alternating periods of tomb and emergence is not to play cat and mouse with us, though while it happens we may feel trapped like a mouse. The real purpose in showing us a little light is to strengthen us for the further purification God wants to do before calling us to emerge. Momentary glimpses of light—intervals of relative calm—are a mercy. During these periods of calm we might think that the night is over. It may be. Or it may only be a lush, well-watered oasis before we are once again pushed out into the hot, dry desert. But at least the oasis gives us a taste of the fertile new land toward which we are headed.

Signs of Emergence

So far I've mostly been using metaphors. But what does emergence actually look like? What signs hint that emergence is happening? While the following signs do not exhaust all the possibilities, and while not all of them will necessarily appear in every person, they suggest some things to look for.

Watch for more receptivity to God. Dark nights open us to God in new and deeper ways. Our sense of emptiness and longing for God is the first hint that our receptivity is expanding. God uses this longing to intensify our dryness so that we soak up the sprinkles of contemplation. As we emerge, even more rain falls. At times contemplation rains on us abundantly enough that we become like a river, fulfilling the promise of Jesus that "out of the believer's heart shall flow rivers of living water" (John 7:38). Our desire for God thus becomes a way for us to become more intimate with God.

Watch for a new sense of friendship with God. Some of us grew up thinking of God as a divine bubble-gum machine: insert your prayer request into the slot, turn the knob of good behavior, and a sweet reward will roll down the heavenly chute into your waiting hands. Numerous people have told me that during their dark night that image of God, and ones like it, went to the garbage dump. They discovered instead that God wants to be our friend. Friendship with God, they learned, does not depend on constantly asking God for forgiveness, on imploring God to do certain things, or even on praising God—although at times our relationship will include each of these. Instead our friendship mainly depends on being with God.

Being with someone is the true food of friendship. Friends do not spend most of their time saying things like, "I'm sorry for all the terrible things I did" (confession) or "Fix this problem for me" (petition) or "You are outstandingly wonderful" (praise). Sometimes friends say those things, but more often they just hang out together. They sit in each other's company, eat together at the same table, take walks together, and enjoy each other. This is the kind of relationship a person emerging from the dark night begins to have with God. Prayer mostly becomes a way of being in God's company—looking at God, listening to God, and loving God. What sustains this friendship more than anything else is contemplation, a way of being with God in love and peace. Jesus called it abiding: "Abide in me as I abide in you. Just as the branch cannot bear fruit by itself unless it abides in the vine, neither can you unless you abide in me" (John 15:4).

Watch for a nearly continual awareness of God, whether the awareness is conscious or semiconscious. To enhance our new and abiding friendship, God grants us a sense of the Spirit's presence that rarely leaves us, unless we enter another dark night. A woman I know passed through several nights in her forties and fifties, one of which included an extended illness and death of a close family member. But in the decades since, her sense of the Spirit's presence has virtually never left her. Her level of Spirit awareness varies, to be sure, but as she goes about her daily work, whether in the kitchen, in the car, or at the store, she knows God is nearby. She not only believes this by faith, but she also senses it deep inside her. For her, the presence of God is palpable.

Watch for new satisfaction, even delight, with contemplation. While the night is still underway, contemplation comes to us in fits and starts, like a summer wind that puffs up and tapers off a few seconds later. When we emerge from the night, the wind on our sails gets steadier. One middle-aged woman went through several dark nights, each of them spaced several years apart, with the latest one the most intense of all. As a result she is now far more adept at recognizing and receiving the infusion of God's peaceful love than she was before.

Watch for a growing awareness of freedom. As God liberates us from some of our attachments, we become freer. Laura, for instance, was liberated from her unhealthy attachment to music. The night did not permanently remove her ability to listen to music, but returned it to her when she was ready to use music in a healthier way. It freed her to appreciate music as it really is, rather than to make unrealistic demands of it.

The night also helps us to extend freedom to others. One pastor who went through an intense dark night of several years emerged and started giving people in the congregation a new level of permission to do what they needed to do and be who they needed to be. "We pastors," he remarked, "can be so controlling, especially in trying to channel a congregation in the way we think it should go. But the night freed me from the need to control everything that happens in the church. Now I'm quite happy to encourage and bless others without controlling them."

Watch for a new spirit of willingness to serve others in the name of Christ or for a new form of service to take shape. Many of us serve others as an outgrowth of our baptism. But sometimes our service is grudging or self-serving rather than genuinely other-serving. After a dark night, however, our service focuses more on other people and less on ourselves. When I finished college, I joined Mennonite Central Committee, the relief and service agency of North American Mennonites, to serve Haitian refugees in southern Florida. At the time I thought I was really serving others. Some of the time, maybe I was. But in retrospect I spent a good bit of those four years looking out for myself and taking care of myself. I hope that the dark nights God has given me since then have made me less self-serving, although I still have a long way to go before I am truly selfless.

Dark nights also stir us to new forms of service. A member of a congregation I once belonged to worked as an accountant in an area business. When a dark night swept through Lance, his sense of alienation from God and the church was so great that he dropped out of congregational life for over a year—much to the embarrassment of his wife and children, who still went to church. The pastor of our church blessed his decision to take a break from church life, with two conditions. First, he wanted Lance not to give up spiritually, but to keep wrestling with God. Second, the pastor wanted to stay in regular contact with him. Lance agreed to both suggestions, and after his dark night ended, he came back to church spiritually renewed, with a holy fire flickering inside him. Within a few months he and his wife decided to become full-time mission workers in an Asian country. After a dark night, some discover an increased desire to work with the poor, to care for the environment, to help reconcile conflict, or to cooperate in some other way with God's mission of shalom. (We will pick this theme up again in chapter 13.)

Finally, watch for a growing life of virtue. Some time ago I attended a multi-day seminar on the dark night led by a group of Christians who each seemed to have gone through one or more intense dark nights during her or his lifetime. I've been to many Christian seminars in the past, but I cannot recall ever being among Christians who seemed to express the fruit of the Spirit (see Galatians 5:22-23) more than these people did. The fruit that particularly impressed me was kindness. When I got home from the seminar, I asked Jenny something of a rhetorical question: "Why are these folks so incredibly kind?" Even as I asked the question, I could guess the answer: through the dark night, God had transformed them, bringing them more deeply into the life of the Spirit.

Thanks to God's hard yet careful work on us during the night (and at other times too), our life looks strikingly more like Jesus'. Our compassion begins to look more like his. Our anger at injustice begins to look more like his (see Matthew 21:12-13). Our passion for peace begins to look more like his. Our focused dedication to God begins to look more like his. Our life takes on a cruciform character.

Mother Teresa

At first glance it may appear that the well-known case of Mother Teresa illustrates an exception to the emergence that comes after the dark night. Certainly her story is extraordinary. The winner of the 1979 Nobel Peace Prize, Mother Teresa was famous for her emphasis on loving others, particularly the poor and dying, as an expression of a larger love for Christ. But what was rarely known during her lifetime is that she actually lived in a dark night for the last fifty years of her life. As far as we know, she was still experiencing the dark night when she died in 1997.

Yet many of the signs of emergence that we've looked at in this chapter—receptivity to and friendship with God, a growing degree of freedom, a willingness to serve others in the name of Christ, and a growing life of virtue—all characterized Mother Teresa's life. Moreover, her private letters reveal not only the pain she felt over her sense of being abandoned by God, but also her growing realization that God was paradoxically using the dark night to create something new and beautiful. As early as 1961, she even wrote about coming to love the darkness as a gift that connected her in a special way to Jesus. Her dark night clearly shaped her spirituality and ministry in profound ways.[19]

A Cycle of Nights

In the last four chapters, the story of Laura has been our main window into how the dark night might develop. The night arrived in her late teenage years and continued into young adulthood, but it can just as easily arrive at age twenty-nine or forty-two or sixty-seven. Later in this book we will consider the stories of people who were given a night later in life.

Mother Teresa seems to have had only one, very long dark night during the course of her life, although occasionally she did experience short reprieves. However, God does not always give us only one dark night during our lifetime. Indeed, God may give us several that we cycle through over the course of our life, always with the purpose of purifying additional attachments, deepening our friendship with God, and enhancing our mission. Each time we will be able to love God and others with a little more of our heart, soul, mind, and strength (see Mark 12:30). And each time, the light of God will shine a little brighter.

—7—

RESPONDING TO THE NIGHT

But we have this treasure in clay jars, so that it may be made clear that this extraordinary power belongs to God and does not come from us. We are afflicted in every way, but not crushed; perplexed, but not driven to despair; persecuted, but not forsaken; struck down, but not destroyed; always carrying in the body the death of Jesus, so that the life of Jesus may also be made visible in our bodies. For while we live, we are always being given up to death for Jesus' sake, so that the life of Jesus may be made visible in our mortal flesh.

—2 Corinthians 4:7-11

You may wonder how to live through a dark night. Since the dark night is one of God's various tools for developing spiritual maturity, how can we cooperate with God's actions during the night? Which attitudes and practices hinder God's work, and which ones help?

When Paul wrote the passage above, he was probably thinking about the religious opposition and physical hardships that he and other early Christians suffered. Yet his words also describe our spiritual suffering during the dark night. Few things make us feel our clay-like nature more than the afflictions and perplexity of the dark night. How do we live while we are "being given up to death" for the sake of transformation? How do we remain open to God during this inner crucifixion while wending our way to resurrection?

What Probably Won't Help

Going back to the way things were. When a dark night surrounds us, we might want to go back to the way our spiritual life used to be. We'd like to reset the clock to an earlier time and return to an era when God seemed closer, prayer seemed easier, and Christian faith seemed more rewarding, if not exciting.

Of course we cannot go back in time. All we can do is live in the present to the best of our ability, trusting that God is just as near and real as God was in former times. Trying to preserve some glorious past simply will not work in a dark night. The point of a dark night, after all, is that the past was not really as glorious as we thought it was at the time. In the past we worshipped false idols without realizing how attached we were to them. In the past our spiritual practices fed and watered us, but now more adequate food—a feast, actually—is spread out on God's table, waiting for us to pull up a chair and eat. In the past our image of God may have provided some comfort, yet that image was less than the fullness of God. So in the dark night God is pushing us ahead to a new life; but before we can get there, some of our old life needs to die.

Trying harder. Some responses to the night skirt close to failure. One of these is to try harder. One woman used to study the Bible inductively several times a week. After choosing a passage, she would ask herself when in biblical history this passage was probably written and what we know about the historical context. She figured out who was speaking in the passage and who was being spoken to. She isolated the main point of the passage and its corresponding subpoints. She identified what the passage wants us to believe or do. Finally she connected the passage to other parts of the Bible. These questions, so important for inductive Bible study, fit well into the pathway of meditation. For many years my friend found meaning and satisfaction in this way of studying Scripture. It nourished her as she walked the path of discipleship.

When she entered a dark night, inductive Bible study became drudgery. She changed nothing about her technique, yet it no longer gave her meaning or satisfaction. So she tried harder. Instead of studying the Bible three times a week, she studied it every day, hoping that, by doing more of it, the sense of God's presence would return to her. But it did not. If anything, she told me later, it seemed that God was getting further away. She was deeply frustrated.

Another friend tried doing the same thing with prayer. For years his usual pattern had been to rise early in the morning, make a cup of coffee, and sit cross-legged on the floor in front of the living-room sofa for a half-hour of mental prayer—a form of meditation where we think sentences and images in our minds, usually without saying anything out loud. For the first ten minutes of these prayer periods, he thanked God for the dawning of another day and for God's mercy, love, and faithfulness. For the next ten minutes he switched to intercessory prayer for others, praying for his wife and children, his colleagues at work, members of his church, officials of his local government, and world leaders. In the final ten minutes he petitioned for himself, inviting God to work in him during the coming day. This pattern of praise, intercession, and petition nourished my friend's faith. On most mornings he stood up from the floor eager to get at the day's activities.

When he entered a dark night, his eagerness for the day dropped away. Not only was the whole half-hour of prayer flat, but his morning cup of coffee tasted flat too. So he tried harder, lengthening his morning prayer to forty-five minutes, giving him fifteen minutes for each movement of praise, intercession, and petition. But the eagerness did not return, and it took great effort to drag himself through the forty-five minutes.

Instead of trying harder, I suggest that you take a Sabbath from the particular form of meditation that no longer works for you. As any carpenter knows, continuing to pound on a bent nail usually bends the nail even more. The better approach is to put the bent nail aside and get a new nail. During a dark night, God wants us to set aside the "bent" practices of meditation that no longer work for us and to find new spiritual practices that are more contemplative.

This doesn't mean that during the dark night we stop praying, reading the Bible, or worshipping. No matter what turns our journey of faith takes, we should still carry prayer, the Bible, worship, and service in our backpack. But the ways we pray, read the Bible, worship, and serve others will change during the night. Instead of only praying with words, we may be drawn to praying without words. Instead of only reading the Bible analytically, we may be drawn to letting the words sink deep into our hearts. Instead of worshipping God only in music and speech, we may be drawn to worshipping God in silence.

Snapping out of it. Occasionally a friend or family member might urge you just to snap out of it. "Get out of whatever funk you're in," they say, "and move on with your life." Such advice is easy to give and impossible to follow. You will not be able to snap out of a dark night, even if you try. One response to a person who offers this advice might be, "I'm sorry, I don't think I can snap out of it. I suspect that God wants me to be in this darkness right now and that God is doing some important things to change me into the image of Christ, even though I'm not sure what those things are. I also believe that this dark night will end when God is finished doing whatever God wants to do in me right now."

One habit of the heart we learn in a new way during the dark night is to release ourselves into God's care. Like a brilliant, top-flight surgeon who performs precise, delicate surgery in the operating room, the Spirit operates on us during the dark night in skillful ways. In the operating room during surgery, we aren't aware of what a surgeon is doing. Likewise we usually cannot see or feel what the Spirit is doing for us during a dark night. Only afterward do we understand better what the operation accomplished. We can trust our plans, dreams, fears, worries, and future to God—who is, after all, the best surgeon of the spirit anywhere in the world.

Refusing. If we want, we can refuse to accept the night. We certainly have the freedom to say, "No, God, I do not want this dark night. Please take it away. I do not want to go through all this dryness and this intense longing for you." Because God respects our freedom, God might honor our request and take the dark night away—for now. But even if God removes the night, God could still take us to another dark night later.

When I was in elementary school, my parents bought my first bicycle and took me to the alley behind our house to teach me this new form of travel. By then I was an expert walker but knew nothing about riding a bike. The first time I got on the bike I fell down and scraped my knee. It hurt so much I refused to ride any more that day. But Mom and Dad persisted in getting me to ride that bike. A few days later I was more ready to endure the pain of another fall, because the benefits of bicycling appealed to me. With enough exposure and practice, I eventually became a good rider.

God similarly persists with us. When the dark night begins, we already know how to get around in the spiritual life with meditation. As God introduces contemplation, a new form of travel, the possibility of scraped elbows and knees might scare us off. We might refuse, and God might say okay, not now. But God will probably be looking for another opportunity to train us in the ways of contemplation. If God grants you a dark night, I hope you eventually say yes, because the effects of contemplation are deep and satisfying.

Giving up. It's extremely tempting in the dark night to give up and walk away from God. We feel so jilted that we want to give tit for tat and jilt God right back.

Please don't do it. Keep turning toward God, even when it seems to you that God is gone. God is *not* gone. God is there and has never stopped loving you, even though you cannot sense that love right now. Do whatever it takes to keep some kind of relationship with God. If you feel like complaining to God, go ahead; God can handle it. If you can't manage anything else, at least yell and scream at God—that's far better for your soul than heaving God into a ditch somewhere along the road and never coming back. The prophet Jeremiah yelled at God and suffered no negative consequences: "O LORD, you have enticed me, and I was enticed" (20:7). Some people have pointed out that the Hebrew word for *enticed* could also be translated as *raped*: "O LORD, you have raped me, and I was raped." Jeremiah does not mean this literally, of course, but figuratively. To accuse God of faithlessness using such extreme language shows we can be honest with God about our feelings. If Jeremiah could use harsh language while talking to God—without incurring any punishment from God— then you and I probably can too.

What Helps During the Night

Pursue God with your desire. One of the best responses to the dark night is to pursue God with your desire. Since God wants first place in our lives, few things please God more during the night than to see us in hot pursuit. Our love for God excels when we allow nothing less than God to satisfy us. Let the desire for God fill you and lead you into new forms of spiritual practice. If you are drawn to build a fire on winter evenings and sit in front of your fireplace doing nothing more than watching the flames leap, then do it. If you yearn to walk in nature, do that. If you feel compelled to write poetry, to paint, or to dance, do so. I don't write poetry and never learned to dance, but I am familiar with paint and paintbrushes. For a while during one of my dark nights, a compelling urge pushed me to express on canvas what I was experiencing. Using black and yellow paint, I ended up creating a series of three paintings that were spiritually cathartic and centered me into peace. God can use such activities to begin teaching us contemplation.

Our thirst for God during the dark night is itself a powerful form of prayer.

> As a deer longs for flowing streams,
>   so my soul longs for you, O God.
> My soul thirsts for God,
>   for the living God.
> When shall I come and behold
>   the face of God? (Psalm 42:1-2)

This thirst tugging at our hearts throughout the day is a gift from the Spirit that teaches us to pray beyond words—and praying beyond words is a crucial feature of contemplation. Our desire for God, even if we do not verbalize it, is one of the most faithful expressions of prayer known to humanity. Our intense passion for God elevates God to the highest priority.

Seek silence and solitude. While going about your daily activities, seek as much silence and solitude as you can. Depending on the kind of person God made you to be, you may need somewhat more, or somewhat less, silence and solitude than another person in the dark night. At some points during your night, you may crave more silence and solitude than at other times. Your daily responsibilities may also affect how much silence and solitude you can get. A receptionist in a busy office, for example, will not have the same opportunity for quiet that a retired widower has. Finding silence can be hard in today's noisy world, but if you are like most people in a dark night, you will quickly discover that being in a quiet environment improves your disposition. Stillness makes you more receptive to the inflow of God's love and more aware of its effects in your life. Although God can send us the gift of contemplation at any moment of the day, we're more likely to receive it while driving a car down a country road with the radio off, for example, than while sitting in a bustling airport terminal.

Seeking silence is more important during the dark night than going out of your way to serve other people. Of course serving others in the name of Christ always pleases God, and if we have ongoing service commitments, we can continue them during the night. But the dark night is a special time when God's immediate goal is to teach us the new pathway of contemplation—and we are more likely to learn it effectively when our surroundings are quiet. As we will see in the next chapter, an increasing desire to serve others usually happens *after* the dark night is over. But *during* the night, God is more interested in training us to receive this infusion of love and peace. Allow yourself to revel in silence and its cousin, solitude.

Stay connected to other Christians. This suggestion may sound as though it contradicts what I just said about seeking solitude, but community is as important as solitude. Like solitude and silence, staying connected in some way with the larger body of Christ is a crucial survival tool during the dark night. Keep going to worship, even when you don't get much out of it. Let the congregation's prayers carry you when you cannot pray in ways that make sense to you. Allow their singing to sustain you when you cannot sing. Permit their companionship to represent for you the unfailing companionship of Christ. Let their witness in the world reassure you that hope has not failed and that God's mission in the world continues even while you remain in a dark night. If staying in your current congregation is more than you can bear, at least find another congregation where you can be connected to Christ's people.

Also stay connected to your friends, particularly your Christian friends, who can be lifesavers during a dark night. Likely not all of them will be familiar with the dark night or understand what you are going through. But perhaps one or two of them can at least listen as you talk about your experiences. If you happen to have a friend who has lived through a dark night, you are especially fortunate. Such a friend might offer suggestions for sustaining yourself during this trying time.

Develop skills to navigate at night. Take a cue from the animal world and develop ways to navigate in the night. Many animals have adapted to living in the dark. Some bats have echolocation for navigating in deep darkness and catching insects while flying. Some species of moles are blind but have sensitive noses that help them to flourish underground in utter darkness. Owls, mice, and cats have special eyes that permit them to spot food between sunset and sunrise.

In contrast to these nocturnal animals, we are diurnal, spending most of our waking hours in the daylight. Still, we can walk outside at night and adapt to darkness. As the pupils of our eyes widen, we start to notice objects that can be seen only in darkness, such as stars and the flashing of fireflies.[20] Our other senses also adapt to darkness: when our eyesight no longer dominates, we hear sounds we don't normally hear and smell fragrances we might not have noticed otherwise. The night helps us to perceive realities that we normally miss in the daytime. We learn to love the gifts of the darkness.

Similarly, we can adapt to a spiritual dark night. When the spiritual senses we relied on before the night no longer work so well, we can compensate by allowing other spiritual senses to become stronger. We sense new things that we never paid attention to before. For instance, we may discover that we now have an awareness of sin that we never noticed before, or noticed only in a superficial way. A more acute sense of our sin usually makes us feel that we're not making much spiritual progress. We might verge on despair over the state of our relationship with God, questioning whether we're really making much progress toward holiness. But our assessment about that is wrong because seeing the depth of our own sin is a necessary condition for growing in holiness. God is helping us to realize in a new way how often our own efforts fail and how much we need the Spirit's transformative power. In the long run, seeing the extent of our sin humbles us. This too is a great gift.

Find a contemplative prayer practice. Cultivating a new practice of contemplative prayer is an excellent response to the night. In addition to Taizé-style services, centering prayer, the Jesus Prayer, walking the labyrinth, or *lectio divina* (all discussed in chapter 5), you might try other contemplative practices.

My family and I recently kayaked on a quiet lake in Wisconsin early one morning when almost everyone else was still in bed. The rugged cliffs, stately trees, and calls of towhees that we met along the way put us all into a contemplative spirit that considerably improved our moods and relationships with each other. Canoeing or fishing, when done in a quiet environment with openness to the wonder of God, can also become prayerfully contemplative. If boating doesn't interest you, consider looking lovingly and for an extended period at a natural object from God's creation, such as a flower, a stone, or a leaf. Gardening functions as contemplative prayer for some people.

Others have discovered that praying with icons leads them into a quiet receptivity that permits God's love to flow into them. Looking at icons as an aid to contemplative prayer has a long, carefully crafted history in the Christian church, so much so that icon painters have developed special techniques, such as drawing elongated hands and enlarged eyes that invite us to a spiritual way of seeing. Reproductions of Russian and Greek icons are readily available on the internet or in art books at your local public library. When you find a particular icon that appeals to you, look gently at it for at least five to ten minutes, longer if you have time. Let your eyes rest on the icon's detail that most interests you; this may be the eyes, the face, or the hands of the figure represented on the icon. Then let your prayer flow from what you see and what is evoked within you. If prayer in the conventional sense isn't possible, then just continue looking, which itself can be a form of prayer.

Find a spiritual director. If you are having a particularly hard time, finding a spiritual director familiar with the dark night can be most helpful. While a spiritual director (sometimes called a spiritual guide) cannot take away your dark night, she or he can walk through it with you and may be able to offer insights along the way that will help you get through some of the rocky terrain. Generally you meet with the spiritual director once a month for an hour to talk about whatever issues you bring for conversation.[21]

Unfortunately, not all spiritual directors thoroughly understand the dark night. The ideal spiritual director is well trained in the Bible, theology, and spiritual direction, and is also experienced in the dark night. When you contact a spiritual director, you can ask what kind of training and experience he or she has had, especially with the dark night, and if you prefer someone with more training or experience, simply keep looking. If you're already meeting with a spiritual director who doesn't know much about the dark night, you can, of course, consider whether to switch directors. But even if your current director is not familiar with the dark night, you might still decide to stay with her or him if you've been meeting together for some time and have established a good relationship. Your director might have strengths in other areas that you value highly.

If necessary, seek professional help for depression. While a dark night is underway, some people also have depression. In 2005, as part of a qualitative research project, I interviewed fifteen people about their experiences of the dark night. Slightly more than half of them—nine people—had also been treated for depression, with both medication and talk therapy, at some point during their dark night. For seven of these people, the dark night began and ended at different times than the depression began and ended. For the remaining two people, the dark night and depression began and ended at virtually the same time.

Seventy-eight percent of these people thought that their experience of the dark night was distinctly different from their experience of depression, even though their experiences of night and depression had overlapped for at least several months. One of them said, "I had been depressed some years ago and know what that was like. But this dark night that I'm in now seems different; and the longer the night lasts, the more convinced I am that the two are different phenomena."

Professionals who are familiar with both the dark night and depression agree they are different. As far as I know, only two qualified writers in the English language have published information on the relationships and differences between depression and the dark night. One is Gerald May, a psychiatrist who in his later years began practicing the ministry of spiritual guidance and worked with a number of people in the dark night. In *The Dark Night of the Soul: A Psychiatrist Explores the Connection Between Darkness and Spiritual Growth*, a book he wrote just before he died, May observed that, while people often experience a dark night and depression simultaneously, each condition is different and calls for different responses. Depression calls for a psychiatric response, he says, and the dark night calls for a spiritual response.[22]

The other writer is Kevin Culligan, a psychotherapist and spiritual director who has written a detailed essay on the similarities and differences between the dark night and depression. He agrees with May that the two are different phenomena that can appear in the same person either simultaneously or independently of each other. Like May, he urges depressed people to see a psychiatrist and recommends spiritual guidance for people in a dark night.[23]

Because I have no training in psychiatry or psychology, I am not qualified to diagnose depression, but given that the dark night and depression sometimes overlap, I hope you will see a doctor or a psychiatrist for an evaluation if you think you might be depressed. Depression can seriously hamper our ability to function at home, work, and school. More than in the past, depression is also a treatable illness in many cases. According to the website of the Depression and Bipolar Support Alliance, depression may stem from genetics, biochemistry, or a variety of other factors. The symptoms of depression can include

- prolonged sadness or unexplained crying spells;
- significant changes in appetite and sleep patterns;
- irritability, anger, worry, agitation, anxiety;
- pessimism, indifference;
- loss of energy, persistent lethargy;
- feelings of guilt, worthlessness;
- inability to concentrate, indecisiveness;
- inability to take pleasure in former interests, social withdrawal;
- unexplained aches and pains;
- recurring thoughts of death or suicide.

Mental health professionals urge you to see your doctor for an evaluation and for a review of your family's history if you experience five or more of these symptoms for more than two weeks or if any of these symptoms interfere with your work or family activities.[24]

In contrast to the symptoms of depression, three signs suggest the presence of a dark night. All three must be present at the same time:

- a sense of dryness in your spiritual life;
- a difficult time praying in your usual way, sometimes even an inability to pray the way you once did;
- a growing desire to be alone in loving awareness of God.

How, then, does depression differ from a dark night? Further research needs to be done on this important question, particularly since many Christians now have a basic understanding of depression while fewer know much, if anything, about the dark night. But based on the work of May and Culligan, I offer the following preliminary chart that shows how the two can differ, given the state of our research.[25] This chart will be less useful, however, for people who are experiencing both depression and a dark night.

People with depression may ...	People in a dark night may ...
Eat and sleep with difficulty	Eat and sleep normally
Lose effectiveness at work, and in extreme cases cannot even get out of bed to go to work	Continue to function creatively and energetically at work
Display bitter or cynical humor	Display humor that sparkles
Be self-absorbed	Have compassion for others
Focus increasingly on self, so that the quality of one's relationship with God may not even seem to be important	Focus increasingly on God, so that the quality of one's relationship with God becomes the main focus of the experience
Sense this condition is wrong and want to change it	Sense this condition is somehow right and would not have it otherwise
Plead for help	Want explanations, but do not plead for help
Fail to display increasing freedom or liberation from lesser gods and goods	Display an increasing amount of freedom, a growing liberation from attachments to lesser gods and goods
Be obsessed with suicide or may intend to destroy themselves	Wish for death in order to be closer to God, but will not attempt suicide
Try to rebuild their life the way it was before the depression	Be ready to relinquish the old self (the "false self") and push ahead to a new self centered in Christ
Make other people feel frustrated, depressed, or annoyed in their presence	Make other people feel graced, consoled, or energized in their presence

If you are living with both depression and a dark night, getting help for the depression may give you more energy to respond to God's actions in your dark night. Treatment for depression will not take away the dark night, but it will help you to be present more fully to the inflow of God's love.

Cultivate poverty of spirit. Finally, we respond well to the dark night if we can cultivate poverty of spirit. The very first words Jesus speaks in the Sermon on the Mount underscore the importance of spiritual poverty: "Blessed are the poor in spirit, for theirs is the kingdom of heaven" (Matthew 5:3).

Jesus is not talking here about material poverty (although he has plenty to say about that in other places), but about spiritual poverty. He suggests that when we are poor in spirit the door to the kingdom of heaven swings wide open. Poverty of spirit widens our access to God. Perhaps it is no accident that the Sermon on the Mount begins with these words. By placing this particular beatitude first, the Gospel of Matthew infers that poverty of spirit is crucial for all that comes afterward in the sermon. Being poor in spirit is a necessary ingredient in the Christian life, like flour in bread.

Our best example of spiritual poverty is Jesus himself. In his letter to the Philippians, Paul quotes a hymn that early Christians presumably sang in their worship services and urges his readers to cultivate the same poverty of spirit that Jesus had.

> Who, though he was in the form of God,
>   did not regard equality with God
>   as something to be exploited,
> but emptied himself,
>   taking the form of a slave,
>   being born in human likeness.
> And being found in human form,
>   he humbled himself
>   and became obedient to the point of death—
>   even death on a cross.

Therefore God also highly exalted him,
    and gave him the name
    that is above every name,
so that at the name of Jesus
    every knee should bend,
    in heaven and on earth and under the earth,
and every tongue should confess
    that Jesus Christ is Lord,
    to the glory of God the Father. (2:6-11)

Jesus' act of emptying himself illustrates poverty of spirit. This hymn boldly declares that wonderful things happened after Jesus emptied himself of the rights and privileges of having God's form. While poverty of spirit initially led him to share our human condition and to suffer crucifixion, it also led to an exalted relationship with God.

To illustrate poverty of spirit and the exalted relationship with God to which it leads, Jesus told a story:

> "Two men went up to the temple to pray, one a Pharisee and the other a tax collector. The Pharisee, standing by himself, was praying thus, 'God, I thank you that I am not like other people: thieves, rogues, adulterers, or even like this tax collector. I fast twice a week; I give a tenth of all my income.' But the tax collector, standing far off, would not even look up to heaven, but was beating his breast and saying, 'God, be merciful to me, a sinner!' I tell you, this man went down to his home justified rather than the other; for all who exalt themselves will be humbled, but all who humble themselves will be exalted." (Luke 18:10-14)

Both the hymn in Philippians and the parable in Luke evoke some of what happens to us in the dark night. During the night, the Holy Spirit empties our disordered attachments, which block a fuller relationship with God. In this process of spiritual crucifixion we learn poverty of spirit. We cry out to God for mercy. As we live poverty of spirit, God also exalts us to a new quality of relationship with God. This exaltation is not the same kind of relationship Jesus has with God, and we are not worshipped as Jesus is. Yet the dark night of contemplation does usher us into a new relationship with God that gives us tranquility, love, and joy.

Poverty of spirit is a tree to cultivate and a pear to harvest. At a certain point during the night, God instills poverty of spirit in us without much effort on our part. Sometimes it appears as we recognize how deeply buried sin is in our lives and how much we need God to root that sin out—and yet at the same time we sense that God accepts us as we are, sin and all. At other times a wave of spiritual poverty washes through us when we realize we cannot pray without God's help, act lovingly without God's help, or even breathe without God's help. Or spiritual poverty might settle in when we accept that, for this season of life, God is going to seem distant; such acceptance can give us the ability to be peacefully silent as we wait for God to do what God wants to accomplish. In any of these ways poverty of spirit makes us depend on God and God's mercy. It knits us to God more intimately.

Many times during the dark night I've prayed the words of the tax collector in Luke 18, "God, be merciful to me, a sinner!" In my most desperate moments, when God seemed far away and I couldn't find my way forward, I shortened this prayer to perhaps the simplest, most basic spoken petition any of us can form: "Help!" My soul seemed so empty, my mind so confused, my heart so faint, my hope so thin, that I no longer even knew how to pray. The only word I could find was help. Carried on that word were my deepest longings for connection with God. Poverty of spirit may be the most profound hospitality we can offer God because it creates inner space for God to do the work of exaltation and exultation.

Part 3

THE NIGHT'S OTHER APPEARANCES

—8—

THE DARK NIGHT IN VOCATION

Whom have I in heaven but you?
And there is nothing on earth that I desire
other than you.
—Psalm 73:25

The first section of this book explored the dark night in our life
of prayer. When most people talk about the dark night, they
think about it mainly in this way—as a spiritual experience of our
inner life with God. Yet we also have outer lives in which the dark
night can appear. The next three chapters explore expressions of
the dark night in three areas of our outer lives—work, family and
marriage, and groups such as congregations.

Because human beings are an integrated whole, what effects
one part of our life will usually affect other parts too. We should
not be surprised, consequently, if a dark night appears in several
areas of our life at the same time. For example, some people

simultaneously struggle through a dark night in their marriage and in their prayer life. Others might find a dark night in their local congregation and in their workplace but not in their family or in their personal relationship with God. The dark night can appear in any combination of personal prayer, vocation, marriage or family, and church. It can begin in one area of life, such as prayer, and later expand to another area, such as the workplace. God is merciful, however, and rarely puts us through a dark night in all four areas at once. That would be more than most of us could handle.

An Accountant's Dark Night

Tony is thirty-seven, married to Joyce, a father of three children—and wildly successful at work. After college he joined a public accounting firm in Miami, and years of diligent, accurate work, coupled with a willingness to put in extra hours when a project required it, quickly earned Tony respect from the firm's partners, who rewarded him with regular pay raises. A handsome income allowed Tony and his wife to buy a house in the upscale suburb of Coral Gables. When he landed a large new account for the firm, Tony achieved the dream he had relentlessly pursued since college: he was made a partner in the firm and given a substantial salary increase. The excitement of living his dream, along with a new level of responsibility and a new plush office, kept Tony elated for two months.

Then the elation shifted into what Tony thought was boredom. A few weeks after boredom came disenchantment, and after that gloom, until one Saturday afternoon while sitting on his backyard deck, nursing a glass of iced tea, Tony realized the dream he had worked so long to achieve felt hollow. "For all those years before making partner, I expected that partnership would give me such a huge sense of accomplishment that I'd need nothing more in life," he observed. "But after achieving my dream, I felt aimless. I had no goals left to achieve. I peered ahead into the next thirty years until my retirement and saw only long hours at work doing the same things over and over. For the first time, I realized that the stuff I had acquired over the years—the pool, the BMW, the membership at the country club, the vacation cottage in Wyoming—was making me gloomy instead of joyful."

Several weeks after these musings on his deck, Tony's thoughts turned to God in a new way. Rather than dwelling only on himself and the dissatisfaction he felt, he wondered about the role of God in his life.

Tony had come to faith in college and been baptized his sophomore year. He had joined a Christian fellowship on campus and for a while was enthusiastic about his faith. During his junior year he led a small-group Bible study in the dorm, where he and Joyce met. His infectious enthusiasm persuaded several new members to join the group, and he enjoyed praying aloud, debating questions of faith, and "being in the Word." His and Joyce's excitement for God sustained them through the rest of college.

After he and Joyce married, graduated, and moved to Miami, they joined a local church. In general the church was fine, except they did not feel the same level of spiritual intensity they had felt in college. Maybe it was because they had moved to a different part of the country, started new jobs, and had children. Whatever the cause, they felt less enthusiastic about Christian faith. Tony did develop regular spiritual practices, however. On Monday, Wednesday, and Friday mornings before work, he ran five miles through the neighborhood, repeating silently as he ran the Jesus Prayer ("Lord Jesus Christ, Son of God, have mercy on me"). On Tuesday, Thursday, and Saturday mornings, he read a chapter from the Bible and prayed for his family, his colleagues at work, and various situations in the world.

When the aimlessness and disenchantment settled in after making partner, Tony wondered if he might have committed some awful sin that drove God away. He examined himself carefully over the next month. Had some expression of lust, greed, or envy sneaked into his soul? Had he recently ruptured one of his relationships? Was some other sin lurking in the corner of his life? There was old sin that had always been there, but he could think of nothing new. When he prayed fervently to God to reveal what was wrong, the only reply heaven offered was silence.

One Tuesday morning while reading the eighth chapter of Amos, Tony realized that his problem was God, or rather, the present state of affairs in his relationship with God.

> The time is surely coming, says the Lord GOD,
>   when I will send a famine on the land;
> not a famine of bread, or a thirst for water,
>   but of hearing the words of the LORD. (Amos 8:11)

"'Famine'—that's my problem," he thought to himself. "It doesn't quite feel like boredom. It's more like famine, an absence of words from the Lord. How ironic! I've been extremely successful in my job and have plenty of money. No one in our family has health problems. I've achieved the American Dream. I live in plenty and yet spiritually I'm starving for God. I'll work harder on my spiritual life so the presence of the Lord will return to me."

Determined to pursue God, Tony made several changes. First, he resolved to read two chapters from the Bible on Tuesdays, Thursdays, and Saturdays instead of only one. Second, on Saturday mornings he would spend ten minutes in intercessory prayer rather than the five he normally did. Third, he would call the chairperson of the gifts discernment committee at church to say he'd be willing to work with the youth group if they wanted him to. Surely when God saw how serious he was about reading the Bible, praying for others, and helping out at church, God would reward him with a greater sense of satisfaction at work.

Although Tony implemented all three decisions, God did not satisfy him. If anything, things seemed to get worse. Reading

Scripture was almost as interesting as reading the Miami phone directory, and the extra chapter helped not a whit. His praying was as pleasurable as golfing in thirty-degree weather. And even though his and Joyce's oldest daughter was nearly a teenager, he had a hard time connecting with any teenagers in the youth group at church. Worst of all, he had to drag himself to the office in the mornings, not because he was tired or depressed, but because all meaning had disappeared from his work. It was tempting just to give up and walk away from his Christianity.

As the months passed, he became even less enthusiastic about work at the firm and about all the stuff he and Joyce had bought. Yet he felt trapped. What he had was the dream he had wanted all his adult life. What else could he do; how else could he be? Wasn't accounting in line with God's will? After all, God had given him the skills to excel in that vocation. In many ways the job fit perfectly. So why this discontent? Without knowing what a dark night was, Tony had come into one that started in his vocation and expanded to include his inner spiritual practices.

An Invitation to Let Go

One Saturday in June, Tony was in the leather armchair of his study at home, trudging through those two chapters from the Bible that he had committed himself to read. He began with Genesis 22.

> After these things God tested Abraham. He said to him, "Abraham!" And he said, "Here I am." He said, "Take your son, your only son Isaac, whom you love, and go to the land of Moriah, and offer him there as a burnt offering on one of the mountains that I shall show you." (verses 1-2)

He started reading the next sentence when something fluttered at the edge of his consciousness. He went back to the beginning of chapter 22 and read those verses again. Isaac. Abraham's son. The son he had worked many years to have. The son who, when finally born, gave such huge joy to Abraham and Sarah. Now God was asking Abraham to sacrifice Isaac. Give him up. Isaac the dream. Give up the dream.

Tony sipped his coffee. *Let it go. You said you were disenchanted. Resign.*

His mug abruptly landed on the desk. "No, surely not that!" he whispered. "Not my job! Let it go? Resign? What would I do then?" He whirled his chair around to stare out the window. Let go. Relinquish. Release what he had been grasping so tightly. No! And yet, for the rest of the day, as he puttered around the house, Tony mused about letting go, an ostinato softly repeating on the edge of his awareness. That night when they climbed into bed and Tony told Joyce what had happened, she was incredulous, but did not say no.

Tony and Joyce allowed the question of his employment at the firm to season for several months. They talked to their extended family members, a few trustworthy friends, and their pastor. They prayed. And the longer the process went, the more open they became to the possibility of Tony resigning his job.

That fall Tony was again reading the Bible and flipped to the beginning of the story of Abraham and Sarah, when they were still called Abram and Sarai. "Now the LORD said to Abram, 'Go from your country and your kindred and your father's house to the land that I will show you. I will make of you a great nation, and I will bless you, and make your name great, so that you will be a blessing'" (Genesis 12:1-2).

In that moment it felt like the decision was made. He was ready to go, to resign, without the foggiest idea what might happen next. The fact that God promised to bless Abram and Sarai as they went to a new place gave Tony hope that God would also bless him and Joyce as they went to an unknown future. Joyce agreed to the decision, and that afternoon Tony typed a letter of resignation to the firm.

His colleagues worked hard to change his mind. One called

him a fool. But Tony was resolute, partly because he felt great peace about it. From the moment he finished writing his letter of resignation, he was convinced he had made the right decision. God seemed to be in this.

One evening several weeks later, as Joyce was reading the *Miami Herald,* she saw a small ad in the help-wanted section of the classifieds for a controller at one of the city's larger social service organizations. "Look at this," she said as she handed it to Tony. Something stirred in him as he read the ad. He got his laptop and went to the organization's website. Their mission of serving Haitians, Hispanics, and African-Americans through job training, job placement, and economic development interested him. When he found the job description for the controller, he quickly realized he was qualified, although the salary range was less than half of what he had been making as a partner at the accounting firm. This would mean a significant change in their household spending patterns. But in this job, Tony would be helping low-income people in a way he had not been doing at the accounting firm. Jesus worked with low-income people; and if Tony was a follower of Jesus, maybe this was what God was nudging him to do next.

So he applied—and was hired two weeks later. Given their drastically reduced income, Tony and Joyce realized they would have to move into a less expensive house. Therefore a few months after Tony started working at the social service agency, they sold their home in Coral Gables and moved into a smaller house in Miami Shores, a suburb just north of Miami where the mortgages were considerably lower. To conserve money, he terminated his membership in the Coral Gables country club. They quit shopping at expensive downtown boutiques and went to K-Mart instead. They sold the vacation cabin in Wyoming.

As Tony switched jobs, God's presence seemed to return. His vocation now had the clear purpose of promoting economic development among multiethnic communities. Worship at church, even the sermons, interested him more than at any time since they had moved to Miami. He looked forward to his thrice-weekly Scripture reading and prayer, because the tip of the Spirit's wings often brushed him. Running the other days of the week, praying as he ran, often filled him with exultation. His relationship with God seemed better than it had ever been.

He also noticed that he had more time. Instead of working sixty-five hours a week, he only worked forty-five. Not only did this allow more time for Joyce and the children, it also left more time to be with God in a new way. His new job began at nine in the morning, leaving time to linger in his leather chair at home before going to work. Coffee cup in hand, he looked out the window at the banyan tree straddling the property line with the neighbors. The banyan's aerial roots and multiple trunks endlessly fascinated him and freed his mind to shift into an attitude of humble receptivity before God. When he got up after fifteen or twenty minutes of looking, he felt renewed with God's peace. It was, of course, the practice of contemplation taking root.

More contemplation often happened while riding the High Street bus to work. Freed from the responsibilities of driving in Miami traffic, Tony gazed out the bus window at the stores and palm trees whizzing by, or pondered the many brown faces around him. When his stop came, he stepped off the bus, filled with tenderness for the multicultural population of his city, eager for the day's work. New practices of contemplation were nudging him toward Christlike compassion.

Attachment to the American Dream

Tony's dark night illustrates the softening and eventual dissolving of his attachment to the American Dream. As the night steadily did its work, Tony discovered that he no longer wanted the accouterments of that dream because the dream no longer mattered. What mattered was heeding the Spirit's nudging and following the example of Jesus. Using the tool of the dark night, God dethroned Tony's dream and regained the primary position in his life. The night brought about such radical change in Tony's outer and inner life that we might call it a second conversion experience.

Divestment

The dark night divested Tony of things that did not enhance his long-term spiritual health. In the business world, companies periodically divest themselves of products or services that no longer fit their main mission. A company might divest itself of an unprofitable line of products to concentrate on more profitable ones. A large corporation might divest itself of a whole division that, although profitable, diverges from its core business. Divestment is a normal process that businesses use to make themselves more effective and efficient.

God uses a similar process during the dark night to divest us of things that hinder our core mission, which Jesus defined as loving God with all of our being (see Mark 12:29-30). When we diverge from this mission and start to love other things, God sometimes ushers us into a dark night to strip away spiritually unprofitable parts of our lives. God nudged Tony to divest the trappings of the false self, allowing Tony's true self to emerge. Through divestment God reoriented Tony's vocation to serve people at the bottom rather than at the top of society.

Divestment regularly occurs during the dark night. A vocational dark night might lead us to change positions within the same company or organization, or it might lead us to change the way we think and feel about our current job. A more sweeping change in a vocational dark night could convince us to leave our old vocation and enter a new one. One woman, for instance, left her original vocation of being a lawyer, went to seminary, and became a pastor in a large congregation in the western United States.

What are the signs of a vocational dark night? One sign is that we have a hard time fulfilling the usual responsibilities of our job. The problem is not incompetence; in fact we may continue to be highly competent, even to the point of receiving accolades from our colleagues. Instead the problem is that our work responsibilities seem so pointless, redundant, or tedious that we just go through the motions. We can barely bring ourselves to do what the job requires of us. A second sign is that our work brings us little or no satisfaction. Whether we work in an office, classroom, or factory, it seems we're not accomplishing much that is truly important; what we do has no satisfying purpose. This is not the sense of flatness that happens occasionally to everyone at work, but a persistent impression of emptiness that lasts for months or years. A third sign is that God seems far away from us at work, and yet we deeply wish we could sense God nearby. If all three of these signs are present at the same time, we can suspect that God has given us a dark night in our vocation.

Elijah's Vocation

The biblical story of Elijah demonstrates that the dark night can even come to people who are already engaged in full-time Christian service. Elijah's vocation was to represent God in an ongoing dispute against Ahab and Jezebel, the rulers of Israel. Ahab's first sin was to marry Jezebel, a Sidonian princess, and to spend public funds building a temple for Jezebel's god, Baal, instead of spending that money to aid poor citizens of Israel (see 1 Kings 16:31-33). Jezebel was no wallflower. An unusually powerful queen, she brought 450 prophets of Baal and 400 prophets of Asherah (Baal's consort or wife) into the nation of Israel to promote the Baalite religion (see 18:19). Later Ahab and Jezebel stole a choice vineyard from Naboth, a poor man, earning them God's fierce criticism (see 1 Kings 21).

Appalled by this political administration's behavior, Yahweh imposed a drought on the land (see 17:1). After three years of drought, when Israel was desperate for water and food, Elijah engineered a public showdown against Jezebel's prophets at Mount Carmel. Which god, Baal or Yahweh, would shoot fire from heaven to burn a sacrifice of bulls? Despite outrageous acts of prayer that included cutting themselves with swords, the prophets of Baal received no response. But at a simple spoken prayer from Elijah, Yahweh's fire consumed both the bull and the water that drenched it. Elijah seized the moment, killed all of Jezebel's prophets, and proved to watching Israelites that Yahweh was powerful while Baal was impotent (see 18:20-40).

God never told Elijah to orchestrate this dramatic showdown on Mount Carmel. Nothing in the story says that the contest of bulls or the slaying of Jezebel's prophets were God's wishes. Instead the story suggests that the confrontation on Carmel and the murder of Jezebel's prophets were *Elijah's* ideas. God merely ordered Elijah to present himself to King Ahab to announce that God will finally send rain after three years of drought (see 18:1). The rest—the confrontation on Carmel—was Elijah's doing; and as the story unfolds, God will hint ever so gently that Elijah mistakenly took matters into his own hands.

Elijah's Dark Night

When Jezebel heard that Elijah had publicly humiliated her by killing her prophets, she reacts the way many rulers do when they are humiliated—she vowed revenge:

> Ahab told Jezebel all that Elijah had done, and how he had killed all the prophets with the sword. Then Jezebel sent a messenger to Elijah, saying, "So may the gods do to me, and more also, if I do not make your life like the life of one of them by this time tomorrow." Then he was afraid; he got up and fled for his life, and came to Beer-sheba, which belongs to Judah; he left his servant there.
>
> But he himself went a day's journey into the wilderness, and came and sat down under a solitary broom tree. (1 Kings 19:1-4)

Elijah knew Jezebel was a ruthless politician who would carry out this threat if she could. So he fled south to Beer-sheba, located in the neighboring nation of Judah, where Jezebel's assassins would have a harder time finding him. Despite his victory at Mount Carmel, Elijah despaired because, as long as the queen sat in the palace, she had the power to hire more prophets of Baal. Adding dismay to despair, Elijah thought he was Yahweh's only remaining prophet (see 18:22; 19:10, 14). He felt lonely, discouraged, and tired. Fearing that all his work had been in vain, he wanted to die. "It is enough," he lamented. "Now, O LORD, take away my life, for I am no better than my ancestors" (19:4).

This marked the low point of Elijah's dark night. He felt able neither to continue his vocation nor to receive satisfaction from it. Yet he still wanted to be faithful to God.

During an intense dark night we may yearn for death. Our search for satisfaction and visceral connection with God is so unrewarding that we turn desperately to alternate sources of excitement—a sexual affair, pornography, overeating, shopping splurges, a luxury vacation, or some other unhealthy diversion that on the surface appears to offer satisfaction but in reality turns out to be hollow. The writer of Ecclesiastes tells the story of one person's desperate search for satisfaction in sensual pleasures, all of which accomplished nothing more than chasing wind (see 2:1-11).

Wishing for death can be another expression of this desperate search for contentment. People in a dark night may want to die in order to recover a sense of closeness to God—to escape the dissatisfactions of this life and go to heaven to live in delightful communion with God. I knew a woman who regularly stood up during the sharing in our Sunday-morning worship services and publicly asked the congregation to join her in praying for her own death. She was in good health, lived in a beautiful home, earned a comfortable income, had a loving family, and belonged to a caring church. Yet after her husband died, a dark night so thoroughly engulfed her that she just wanted to "depart and be with Christ" (Philippians 1:23). Like Elijah, she believed that she had no meaningful work left to do. She pined for death.

God's Response

God does not always grant our request. In Elijah's case, God did not let him die, but sent an angel to feed him for the work ahead.

> Suddenly an angel touched him and said to him, "Get up and eat." He looked, and there at his head was a cake baked on hot stones, and a jar of water. He ate and drank, and lay down again. The angel of the LORD came a second time, touched him, and said, "Get up and eat, otherwise the journey will be too much for you." He got up, and ate and drank; then he went in the strength of that food forty days and forty nights to Horeb the mount of God. (1 Kings 19:5-8)

God has many ways of feeding us so that the dark night's desolation does not overwhelm us. As in the case of Elijah, God may send us an unexpected messenger (the Hebrew word for *angel* means "messenger"), such as a friend or an acquaintance, who feeds our soul and gives us strength. God may also feed us in mysterious ways hidden from our sight. Or in response to our pleas for mercy, God may choose to lower the intensity of the night. More often God feeds us by altering our vocation in some way that brings us renewed energy to do what we are called to do. We are strengthened to continue our ministry in the world of work.

God's Gentle Rebuke

After strengthening him for the work ahead, God sent Elijah to Horeb (another name for Mount Sinai), located at the bottom tip of the Sinai peninsula, far to the south of Israel. As Elijah stood on the mountain, a dramatic, rock-busting windstorm blew by, but Elijah realized that God was not in it. Next a dramatic earthquake shook the region, but Elijah perceived that God was not in that either. Then a fire swept through the area, but again, Elijah sensed that God was not in it (see 19:11-12). After all this grand drama, Elijah finally heard "a sound of sheer silence" (verse 12)—and immediately covered his face in humility because he knew this silence bore the awesome presence of Yahweh.

Elijah's mountaintop experience on Horeb subtly critiques his mountaintop efforts on Carmel. On Carmel, Elijah took matters into his own hands, devising a public contest he knew he could win and then using violence to wipe out the opposition. On Carmel, Elijah tried to manage the course of history, to push the king and queen into a corner where they would be forced to quit sponsoring Baal worship and instead start worshipping Yahweh. The story implies that God, whose divine reputation was publicly at stake, humored Elijah's decision to stage a contest and sent fire to consume the watery bull. Yet Elijah's strategy to force the nation into faithfulness quickly proved unsuccessful when the palace struck back and Elijah fled for his life.

On Horeb, God gently rebuked Elijah, teaching him that God's presence and power are not always found in big, dramatic public actions like earthquake, wind, or fire. Instead God is more likely found in the ever-so-subtle sounds of silence. As God was not fully in the fire that swept by Horeb, God was also not fully in the fire that burned the bull on Carmel. On Horeb, God divested Elijah of his attachment to the grand and the dramatic, stripping him of his attraction to violence. On Horeb, God reoriented Elijah to the small, the subtle, and the silent, reminding Elijah that he does not manage history but is only a bit player in a much larger drama that God understands far better than Elijah does.

Once the rebuke was conveyed, God refocused Elijah's vocation and sent him back into the world of work. Elijah was to leave Mount Horeb and head north, where he would quietly anoint three people: the next king of Aram, the next king of Israel, and the prophet to take Elijah's place. These anointings were not to be grand, public acts (they were not coronations), but were to be carried out quietly with relatively few people around (see 19:15-21). Finally, as a sort of by-the-way, God dryly informed Elijah of the small but significant fact that Israel still had one hundred prophets and seven thousand regular folks who refused to kneel to Baal (see verse 18). Therefore Elijah was not alone. He belonged to a large company of God's faithful, countercultural people who resisted the government's pressure to worship so-called gods that are actually no gods at all.

Jeremiah's Vocation

About 260 years after Elijah's public ministry against Ahab and Jezebel, Jeremiah engaged in a similar vocation against the kings of Judah. Jeremiah also protested the worship of other gods and the pursuit of national policies that favored the rich and ignored the poor. While Elijah was never arrested and never experienced much physical suffering, Jeremiah was arrested numerous times throughout his long career, clamped into the stocks overnight (see Jeremiah 20:1-3), thrown into a muddy cistern (see 38:6), imprisoned (see 38:13, 28), and at the end of his life, kidnapped and taken against his will to Egypt, where presumably he died (see 43:5-7). For reasons the Bible does not name, God consistently protected Elijah from political retribution yet regularly allowed Jeremiah to suffer virtually any retribution his many political enemies wanted to inflict on him. Jeremiah experienced the dark night in a physical, bodily way that Elijah did not.

Public Confidence, Private Despair

In public, Jeremiah confidently spoke God's judgment against the government of Judah and the religious leaders who supported it (see 19:1–20:6). But in private, things were quite different. In private moments, Jeremiah railed against the harassment he received from other people. You, he told God, promised to support me when you first called me to this work (see 1:8, 19), but you aren't keeping that promise! Instead "you are to me like a deceitful brook, like waters that fail" (15:18). Jeremiah did not always sense God's sustaining presence. Since political rulers routinely ignored Jeremiah's counsel, his work gave him few rewards, success, or enjoyment. His dark night came amid great suffering and little vocational success. For the most part, Jeremiah's ministry looked like a failure.

The most intense expression of Jeremiah's dark night came in 20:7-18. This frustrated lament, hurled at God in private despair, contrasted sharply with the public proclamations Jeremiah so confidently spoke in God's name. Jeremiah began with the astounding accusation that God had deceived him, deliberately letting him become an object of public ridicule.

> O LORD, you have enticed me,
>   and I was enticed;
> you have overpowered me,
>   and you have prevailed.
> I have become a laughingstock all day long;
>   everyone mocks me. (20:7)

Jeremiah's vocation had trapped him between two unsavory choices: If he obeyed God's call to speak against the government and its supporters, he only received hostility from those in power. But if he tried to avoid the hostility by keeping silent, the inner compulsion to speak would not let him rest in peace. It was a no-win situation.

> For whenever I speak, I must cry out,
>   I must shout, "Violence and destruction!"
> For the word of the LORD has become for me
>   a reproach and derision all day long.
> If I say, "I will not mention him [God], or speak any more
> in his name,"

> then within me there is something like a burning fire
> > shut up in my bones;
> I am weary with holding it in,
> > and I cannot. (verses 8-9)

No one stood by to support Jeremiah. Even people he thought of as good friends tried to trap him.

> For I hear many whispering:
> > "Terror is all around!
> Denounce him! Let us denounce him!"
> > All my close friends
> > are watching for me to stumble.
> "Perhaps he can be enticed,
> > and we can prevail against him,
> > and take our revenge on him." (verse 10)

Although he had no friends, Jeremiah nevertheless chose to believe that God would fight for him. On the strength of that hope he praised God for the only time in this prayer:

> But the LORD is with me like a dread warrior;
> > therefore my persecutors will stumble,
> > and they will not prevail.
> They will be greatly shamed,
> > for they will not succeed.
> Their eternal dishonor
> > will never be forgotten. . . .
> Sing to the LORD;
> > praise the LORD!
> For he has delivered the life of the needy
> > from the hands of evildoers. (verses 11, 13)

Yet Jeremiah couldn't sustain this hope for long, because the dark night quickly surrounded him again. Now he lashed out in anger.

> Cursed be the day
> > on which I was born!

The day when my mother bore me,
   let it not be blessed!
Cursed be the man
   who brought the news to my father, saying,
"A child is born to you, a son,"
   making him very glad.
Let that man be like the cities
   that the LORD overthrew without pity;
let him hear a cry in the morning
   and an alarm at noon,
because he did not kill me in the womb;
   so my mother would have been my grave,
   and her womb forever great.
Why did I come forth from the womb
   to see toil and sorrow,
   and spend my days in shame? (verses 14-18)

Feeling Betrayed

Jeremiah felt betrayed. His own people had arrested, imprisoned, slandered, and abused him. People he should have been able to count on—his friends, his religious and political leaders—were precisely those who opposed him. Human abandonment made him feel that God had also abandoned him. As a psalmist bewailed, sometimes our "familiar friend" (55:13) is the one who betrays us.

Six months into our marriage, I felt betrayed by two of my familiar friends: my wife, Jenny, and God. Shortly after we were married, Mennonite Central Committee, one of the mission agencies of Mennonites in North America, asked me to accept the main leadership job for their work in Haiti. I was ready to accept the invitation and go; but Jenny dragged her feet, largely because no equally clear role emerged for her. She and I debated and struggled, trying to reach consensus on whether to accept or decline. After many weeks of conversation, Jenny unequivocally said no, she would not go to Haiti.

Her refusal pushed me into a vocational and marital dark night. I felt she had betrayed me. Before our wedding I thought we had agreed that we'd eventually enter a term of service with MCC because it fit our vocation of serving others in the name of Christ. When she refused to go to Haiti, my sense of vocation was gone, ripped out of my hands and zipped through a shredder. I had no idea what I would do. The oasis of our marriage turned into forlorn desert.

I further felt that God had betrayed me, because I really believed God was calling me to serve some of the poorest people in the world under the ministry of MCC. I couldn't imagine a more clear-cut expression of discipleship than that. I wanted to know who—God or Jenny—was to blame for messing with my carefully discerned dream. Was God jerking me around, or was Jenny blocking God's will? Or had I misread the signals from God? I was so mad, I could not pray.

That was twenty years ago, and I still don't know who to blame. But it no longer matters. Two years later, I realized that Jenny and God had actually done me a favor. They divested me of a too-narrow understanding of my work in the world. I had rightly discerned my vocation—to serve others in the name of Christ—but I had wrongly discerned how that vocation would be carried out. By a circuitous path, God eventually pushed me into pastoral ministry (work I had long resisted and did not want to do), which for the past two decades has been what God wanted me to do for this period of my life.

A dark night can come whether we are successful or unsuccessful in our line of work, whether we do our jobs well or badly, whether we are well-loved or deeply hated. Dissatisfaction in work or in relationships with people we thought we could trust drives us, like Tony, Elijah, and Jeremiah, to God as our source of sustenance. God may not immediately console us, but biblical faith testifies that God is our only hope. In the words of Simon Peter, when Jesus asked if the disciples wanted to leave him, "Lord, to whom [else] can we go? You have the words of eternal life" (John 6:68). In this way the dark night impels us toward God—which is just what God wants.

—9—

THE DARK NIGHT
IN FAMILIES

> I waited patiently for the LORD;
>> he inclined to me and heard my cry. . . .
> He put a new song in my mouth.
>> —Psalm 40:1, 3

The call came at 7:11 p.m. "This is Officer Zaeder from the county sheriff's department. Am I speaking with Mr. Eric Lenz?"

"Yes."

"Do you have a son named Tom?"

"Yes, what's the problem?"

"I'm terribly sorry to give you this news, Mr. Lenz, but your son has been in an accident on the corner of Potato Creek Road and Route 121. He died at the scene." The deputy sheriff went on to explain that Tom had been riding his motorcycle out in the country and had probably come to a complete stop before starting up again through the intersection, but neither Tom nor the driver of the south-bound Dodge Ram pickup saw each other until it was too late. Maybe it had something to do with the fact that the truck driver did not have his headlights on, even though it was dusk, and that he had just come from the "happy hour" at a local bar.

However the accident happened, the funeral director, after looking at Tom's body, told Eric there were only two good options: either leave the casket closed during the calling hours and the funeral, or simply cremate the body. As a widower, Eric made the decision alone; he chose cremation.

As if his son's gruesome death were not enough, Eric received a second blow on the day of the funeral. After the interment of Tom's ashes, near the end of the fellowship meal at church, Eric's only daughter, Susan, walked up to him and, with her usual blunt tactlessness, informed him that she was leaving her husband of seventeen years. "I'm moving out next week," she said flatly, "and he can keep the kids himself. I'm sick and tired of hearing about the Pittsburgh Steelers and that '77 Camaro out in the garage that he loves more than he ever loved me. I'm outta here."

As soon as Eric got home and sat down in the living room, he burst into tears.

Eric's Dark Night

Initially Eric found solace in Scripture, believing that God would not fail him in the wake of Tom's death and Susan's separation. "For I am convinced that neither death, nor life, nor angels, nor rulers, nor things present, nor things to come, nor powers, nor height, nor depth, nor anything else in all creation, will be able to separate us from the love of God in Christ Jesus our Lord" (Romans 8:38-39).

He also found comfort at church, where he poured out his troubles to friends, especially to the people in his small group. He prayed like mad, not only in the mornings during his devotional time but dozens of times throughout the day: "Christ, help!

Why have all these things happened? Stay with me through this!" And for a while, Christ delivered. As the tears bounced off his shirt, Eric often sensed the tender, wondrous wisps of the Spirit encircling him, sharing his grief.

After a few weeks, the tender wisps vanished. His prayers for help dropped to the floor as soon as they left his mouth. But that didn't keep Eric from hurling angry accusations at God: "I've been faithful to you all my life, a member of the church since I was fourteen. I've never gone out and committed adultery or murder or robbery. I haven't been stingy in giving to the church. Instead I've given you the best of my talents—teaching Sunday school all these years, serving as an elder, and preaching occasionally when our congregation was between pastors. After my wife died, I raised those two children to the best of my ability and loved them from the depths of my heart. Now you took one away and allowed the other to suffer a shattered marriage! What kind of God are you, anyway?" But heaven offered no reply that Eric could sense.

Every morning after the accident, Eric dragged himself to the walnut writing desk in the corner of the living room to study the Bible. As a retired teacher who had immersed himself in the Bible all his adult life, Eric knew the art of Bible study backward and forward. Yet no matter how hard he worked at it, the vitality seemed to have left the Bible's stories, poetry, parables, and letters. He begged God to blow through his life as God's breath breezed through the waiting disciples at Pentecost (see Acts 2:1-4), but God's breath seemed to have fallen still.

Eric lived with similar difficulties at church. For the first time in his life he felt assaulted by the wordiness of worship—words launched through the air landing nowhere, chatter in a sound box. While the sermon bounced off the walls, Eric's mind flitted dully from organ to pulpit to baptistery. Though he stood with the rest of the congregation for singing, he could bring himself neither to sing the notes nor to whisper the words. On the Sunday they sang "Faith of our Fathers," Eric almost retched because God seemed to have fled the universe. In a conversation with his pastor, Eric lamented, "After all this stuff that's happened to me, I doubt that I can ever trust God to be good to me again."

So deep was Eric's distress that for some time he could not bring himself to stay in communication with Susan, the sole remaining member of his immediate family. He found he could not even concentrate very clearly on her difficulties, let alone know how to respond to her. As much as possible he preferred to remain alone in his house, watching the fire burning in his wood stove, yearning for a seemingly absent God whom he no longer knew how to serve or relate to effectively.

An intense dark night had entered Eric's sense of family life. First, his overall sense of family vitality had dried up, giving him no satisfaction. Second, he found it hard to focus on what he could do to help Susan and her husband with their difficulties. Third, although Eric knew that God never leaves or forsakes us (see Psalm 139:7-12; Hebrews 13:5), it felt to him as though God had disappeared. This familial dark night spread into his inner life of prayer, displaying the three typical signs: an overall dryness in his spiritual life, an inability to pray and study the Bible in his normal way, and a yearning to be with God.

To explore further how God may work through a dark night in family life, we turn to the biblical story of Naomi and Ruth.

A Search for Vitality

The book of Ruth begins with a search for vitality. The nuclear family of Elimelech (husband), Naomi (wife), and Mahlon and Chilion (sons), fled their home town of Bethlehem during a famine, their bellies empty (see Ruth 1:1-2). Since the opening verses do not mention God, we might guess that for this family the land of Judah was empty of God's presence. They starved for food, and they starved for communion with God. Finding neither in their homeland, they moved to the neighboring country of Moab. Since Israelites traditionally held Moabites in contempt, the move to Moab suggests that their situation had truly become serious. This family was desperate for new life.

For a while the family found food in Moab, until a second crisis erupted: Elimelech, husband and father, died. Bereft of her husband, Naomi was left with two sons who soon married local Moabite women (see 1:3-4). These marriages carried the promise of new vitality in the form of possible pregnancies and childbirth. Then tragedy struck a third time: Naomi's sons, Mahlon and Chilion, also died (see 1:5). Now Naomi's situation was truly precarious. Without a husband, she had no financial support. Without children, she had no hope of grandchildren and no hope that her family would continue. Her family had dwindled to two Moabite daughters-in-law, both widows. It appeared that this family's search for vitality had come to a dead end. Of the original family, only Naomi was left, and considering what little hope she had from a social and economic point of view, she might as well be dead too.

However, Naomi still had the option of leaving Moab and returning to her hometown of Bethlehem. This option became more appealing when she heard that the famine back home had ended (see 1:6). She may not have had a husband or sons, but maybe she could at least have food.

Unexpected Loyalty

Naomi planned to return to Bethlehem without her Moabite daughters-in-law. The first daughter-in-law, Orpah, did indeed stay in Moab; but the second, Ruth, chose to go with Naomi (see 1:7-15). Ruth left her nation, her culture, her people, and her friends for the sake of Naomi. She would stay with Naomi through thick and thin, until death. Naomi's God would also become Ruth's God.

> But Ruth said:
> "Do not press me to leave you

or to turn back from following you!
Where you go, I will go;
    where you lodge, I will lodge;
your people shall be my people,
    and your God my God.
Where you die, I will die—
    there will I be buried.
May the LORD do thus and so to me,
    and more as well,
if even death parts me from you!" (1:16-17)

Ruth's loyalty is remarkable. While the story says nothing about how she responded to her own husband's death, we may imagine that Ruth felt just as bereft as Naomi did. Perhaps Ruth believed that there was nothing more for her in the land of Moab and that she might as well go with Naomi and start a new life in Judah. Whatever her motivation, for Ruth this was the beginning of a new adventure in God. She essentially converted to the faith of Israel. Although she would remain ethnically Moabite for the rest of her life, in a spiritual sense she became just as much of an Israelite as Naomi herself.

Bitterness and Hidden Hope

Their arrival in Bethlehem stirred up excitement among the village women who still remembered Naomi. But Naomi stopped their rejoicing when she told her old friends to call her Mara, which means *bitter*. She had left town with a husband and sons but returned empty, with no family, no wealth, no means of support—nothing. She blamed God for this. For reasons beyond her comprehension, God had taken away all that once nourished her. Her emptiness was God's fault, making her feel profoundly bitter (see 1:19-21).

Believing that God had abandoned her, Naomi had entered a dark night centered in her family life. She could not relate to her husband and sons, for they were dead, and she found no satisfaction in her current set of relationships. Although she yearned for God's care and goodness, she felt that God was treating her badly. Overwhelmed by feelings of divine abandonment, Naomi could not see what we the readers see: standing right beside her, living in the same household with her, was Ruth, who had promised never to abandon her. Through Ruth's loyalty, God was loyal to Naomi. Through Ruth's companionship, God was a companion to Naomi. God did care for her—and that care was expressed in Ruth. Naomi was blind to the possibilities for new life that Ruth represented; but, in time, Naomi would realize that Ruth was both a person of value and an agent of spiritual transformation.

Like Naomi, we often do not see that someone or something close to us is a sign of God's goodness and will soon play a key role in shifting our dark night into more visible expressions of God's love. During our dark nights, God usually provides us with a person, a spiritual practice, a congregation, a book, a conversation, or something else that not only sustains us but also changes us. The dark night contains God's transformative power, and the means of this transformation is often at hand from a very early stage in our night. For Naomi, the person at hand was Ruth.

Ruth's Initiative

Naomi and Ruth arrived in Bethlehem desperate, without food, income, or husbands who could contribute to household finances. They had to act soon or they would die of starvation. Naomi might normally have been expected to take charge of this situation; since Bethlehem was her hometown, she knew the people, the relationships, and the customs in a way that Ruth did not. Since Naomi was also older, she had more social status than her daughter-in-law. Naomi should have been the one to find a solution.

That's not what happened. Instead, Ruth took the initiative to find food by going to the fields and picking up stray heads of barley that fell to the ground during the harvest. Ruth was the one who decided that this family, now reduced to two widows staring starvation in the face, would not collapse. Naomi did not even offer to help Ruth.

> Now Naomi had a kinsman on her husband's side, a prominent rich man, of the family of Elimelech, whose name was Boaz. And Ruth the Moabite said to Naomi, "Let me go to the field and glean among the ears of grain, behind someone in whose sight I may find favor." She said to her, "Go, my daughter." So she went. (Ruth 2:1-3)

Inability to Focus

A characteristic difficulty of the dark night is an inability to concentrate on details. Naomi could not pull herself together to focus on doing the things necessary for survival. We may find it difficult to plan an upcoming vacation, a remodeling project in the bathroom, or a special dinner for guests. Our wandering minds will not focus on what we want to focus on.

This inability to concentrate on details during the dark night is not the same as being distracted by the noise of the neighbor's lawnmower or by worry over tomorrow's meeting at work. When we sit down to plan that vacation or dinner party, it may be perfectly quiet in the house and we may not be worrying about anything at all. Yet our mind can't seem to stay on task. We search for airfare on the internet and then can't remember what the amount was after we exit the browser. We look through the cookbook for a new recipe, and soon the fourth recipe gets confused with the fifth and the seventh recipes so that we can no longer keep them apart in our mind. Perhaps we notice a similar lack of focus at work: in a staff meeting we can't recall what a colleague just said, or on the phone we barely follow along as a customer explains her problem. It can be quite humbling to ask someone to repeat what they just said because we're having a hard time focusing. It can be frustrating to fix a computer problem when we can't stay with a line of thought long enough to diagnose the cause. People might wonder if we're losing our competence.

When events like these occur, the source of our difficulty is probably a growing urge for contemplation. The Holy Spirit is gently drawing us away from the normal activities of our lives so we can better receive the inflow of God's love, peace, and delight. Instead of focusing on the details of a conversation or a project, we wish we could just sit quietly in a comfortable chair, looking at nothing, doing nothing, and thinking about nothing in particular. Such a desire may really be a desire for contemplation.

The best course of action in this situation is to take a little time each day to honor the Spirit's call to do nothing except quietly receive what God wants to give you. After a few weeks or a few months, maybe a little longer, you should be able to focus a little better on details once again. The call to contemplation will not diminish, but your attention to detail will improve. If you are fortunate like Naomi, you will have someone like Ruth who can attend to the details for you.

Ruth seemed to realize that Naomi was unable to find solutions to their desperate situation. She therefore took initiative to devise and execute a plan to get food. Her plan turned out to be much better than she had anticipated, since without knowing it she ended up gleaning in a field owned by Boaz, a wealthy relative of Naomi's dead husband (see 2:3-7).

Boaz's Kindness

Word got around fast in a tiny village like Bethlehem (which may have had a population of only three hundred to five hundred people), so it came as no surprise that Boaz had already heard about Naomi and Ruth. Boaz probably also knew they were on the verge of starvation, so he asked Ruth to stay in his field (likely so she would not be molested by men in other fields), and when she was thirsty, to drink from his water jugs (see 2:8-12). Thanks to his kindness, Ruth's labor in the hot sun was handsomely rewarded at the end of the day with a full ephah (about two-thirds of a modern bushel) of barley. Naomi was so impressed by all this food that she seemed to come "out" of the dark night momentarily, and when she learned that Ruth worked in Boaz's field, she praised God for the first time in the story.

> Then Naomi said to her daughter-in-law, "Blessed be he by the Lord, whose kindness has not forsaken the living or the dead!" Naomi also said to her, "The man is a relative of ours, one of our nearest kin." Then Ruth the Moabite said, "He even said to me, 'Stay close by my servants, until they have finished all my harvest.'" (2:20-21)

An End to Naomi's Dark Night

By the end of the book of Ruth, Naomi's dark night had dissolved. Ruth romanced Boaz, who agreed to marry her (see 3:1-11), and they had a son named Obed, who would become the grandfather of King David (see 4:13-17). This family, which had long been desperate for vitality, finally received economic stability and descendants. In Naomi's dark night, God strengthened her perseverance, coaxing her to trust even when the night threatened to undo her. Through the kindnesses of Ruth and Boaz, God showed kindness to Naomi.

> I am about to do a new thing;
> > now it springs forth, do you not perceive it?
> I will make a way in the wilderness
> > and rivers in the desert. (Isaiah 43:19)

Suffering and the Dark Night

Naomi's dark night started with a series of external losses of family, food, and economic security, all of which brought her significant physical and mental suffering. God did not in any way cause this suffering; but God was with Naomi through her suffering, especially in the person of Ruth. Though God did not bring about Naomi's external suffering, God did use the physical and mental suffering that life threw her way as an opportunity to give her the gift of a dark night.

Earlier in this book I tried to illustrate the dark night with stories of people who were not suffering in any significant way. I did this to show that the dark night can come to people who are outwardly successful and experiencing no external suffering. But the dark night can also come to people in deep suffering, such as Naomi, and in the beginning of this chapter, Eric. Suffering, in fact, can prepare the ground for a dark night to sprout. This does not mean that all suffering automatically leads to a dark night; some of our suffering remains just that and never morphs into a dark night. Yet our suffering can lead to a dark night if we and God allow it to.

To say it another way, any form of deep suffering that life throws at us—death of a spouse or a child, inability to conceive, loss of a job, terminal illness, rape, famine, war, AIDS, terrorism, or a tsunami or a hurricane—can help to create the conditions in which we cannot pray or carry out other spiritual practices in our usual way, in which we find little or no satisfaction in life, and in which we yearn for a God who seems to be somewhere in the next galaxy. The dark night can come whether we are failing or succeeding, whether we are poor or rich, whether we have a hard life or a comfortable life, whether we are in physical pain or no pain at all. The dark night is a way to engage God in the middle of our suffering, but not all our suffering is a dark night.

The Dark Night in Marriage

By telling the stories of Eric and Naomi, I do not mean to say that all dark nights in family life come on the heels of suffering. Some people can enter a familial dark night without any outward expression of suffering. Consider the dark night in marriage, which can come in a variety of forms. One spouse, for example, can go through a dark night while the other does not. In this scenario, the best course of action for the spouse who's not in the dark night is to listen to the spouse who is, and to wait patiently for the Holy Spirit to accomplish whatever changes and transformations God wants to achieve. Waiting can last quite a while. I've known some spouses to wait as long as ten to twelve years for God to complete a dark night in their husband or their wife. This can get frustrating if the partner who is in the night wants more silence and solitude than normal, while the other partner wishes for more sounds (such as music) and friends (such as parties).

In a second scenario, both spouses can go through a dark night at the same time. When this happens, things can get rough. For several years, Maria and Ramón unsuccessfully tried to have a child. The first problem was their sheer inability to conceive. For two years they tried every month, charting cycles, taking temperatures, the works—and nothing happened. In the third year they finally managed to conceive. But two months into the pregnancy, the bleeding started. At the hospital, the doctor told them their child had been miscarried. They kept trying, and in the fourth year conceived again. The second month of the pregnancy passed, then the fifth, and the seventh. In the eighth month, while Maria sat at her desk paying bills, she suddenly felt something go wrong inside her, and then all movements in her womb stopped. The next day she went to the doctor, whose staff did an ultrasound and discovered that the baby was dead. They induced labor and Maria birthed a dead son.

Afterward Maria and Ramón wrote a letter to friends in another city.

> We want a living, perfectly healthy child, not a dead one. Plain and simple. We have begged God for a child every way we know how to beg. We've prayed once a day, five times a day, out loud and in silence, through bitter and angry tears, prayed for years on end, banging on the door of heaven until our hands hurt. And we don't hear a single thing back from God. We're tired of petitionary prayer because it doesn't seem to do any good.
>
> We're stuck. We now believe that we're not going to get

what we want. We're exhausted physically and spiritually from trying so hard (especially Maria). Somehow we think we're going to have to get by without a child. It's not what we want; it's not what we dreamed of; but we don't know what else to do; and even if we did, we don't have the energy to do it anymore. Our life feels like a squeezed lemon, ready to be dropped in the garbage.

Ramón and Maria stayed in this squeezed place for quite a while. During this time they began to practice centering prayer twice a day and joined a small group of other pray-ers for support and encouragement. Doing centering prayer for several years slowly unfolded them to the reality of God's power and love. This emerging sense of God's nearness in turn gave them a renewed sense of mission. They decided to become foster parents. Soon after they started talking with child and family services about becoming short-term foster parents, they received their first child, a six-year-old boy. God did not cause their childlessness, but God used it as an opportunity to grant a dark night that eventually led Maria and Ramón to a new mission of compassion, one they had not earlier imagined themselves doing. The dark night and its resulting growth in contemplation changed their lives.

In a third scenario, a dark night can center primarily on the marriage relationship itself, rather than primarily on one or both partners. In this case the wife and husband do not so much sense the dark night inside themselves, but between them. As any married couple knows, there is you and me, but then there is also our relationship—and a marital dark night can sometimes appear in that relationship. The old patterns of spirituality (particular types of prayer, Bible study, service, hobbies, recreational activities, or whatever) that sustained the marriage no longer appear to work. Both partners sense that the relationship is not as satisfying as it used to be. They hunger for a fresh outpouring of the Spirit in their marriage—not for mere renewal of the old that used to be, but for a new quality of relationship they have never had before.

This often happens after a couple's children grow up and leave home. Of course a dark night can happen at any point in a marriage, but it seems to occur with some frequency at the empty-nest stage. The children who had been the focus of the marriage for perhaps twenty to thirty years are now gone. During those years, nurturing the spirituality of children shaped much of the parent's own spiritual practices. To model faith in Christ, many parents engage in practices of meditation (such as vocal prayer and inductive Bible study) because those are precisely the spiritual practices children understand most easily and need to learn if they are to start off right. The family's congregation supplements this religious training through the many expressions of meditation that most churches use in worship and Christian education classes.

But once the children leave, or even once they enter their middle to late teen years, parents may find themselves thirsting for something in addition to meditation. Reading a Bible storybook aloud, reciting a rote prayer before meals, or taking a yearly family service trip might no longer nourish the marriage the way it did when the children were there to participate. At this point, husband and wife want to find new patterns of spiritual nourishment, which for most couples will mean developing contemplative practices that open them to the infusion of God's shalom.

This phenomenon may partly explain why some empty nesters no longer find traditional Christian education classes appealing. Most adult Sunday school classes use the pathway of meditation, which continues to work well for many people—but not for everyone. Classes with a contemplative focus will probably work better for adults who have been through a dark night, and if their congregation offers no classes like that, some adults may simply skip Christian education classes entirely.

A dark night can create far-reaching changes in family life. It tends to make us more compassionate, more inclined to work with suffering people, more generous in sharing our resources, and more unified with our spouse and children, if we have them.

A dark night may also reconfigure our family in unexpected ways. Consider what happened to Naomi and Ruth by the end of the story. Their new family didn't even come close to our idealized notion of "family" that has a father, a mother, and two kids. The newly constituted family at the end of the book of Ruth was what we would now call a blended family: a widowed grandmother, her widowed daughter-in-law from another ethnic background who is now married for the second time, the second husband, and a newly born grandson who is not genetically related to the grandmother—all living together in the same household.

Eric's Transformation

Earlier in this chapter we left Eric in the throes of a severe dark night mixed with the grief anyone feels who has just lost a son in a traffic accident and watched a daughter choose to leave her husband. To deal with his grief in more useful ways, Eric joined a grief support group in town two months after the accident. The six-month anniversary of Tom's death was hard, as were the one-year and two-year anniversaries; but with time, the grief no longer undid Eric.

The dark night took him on a different course. At the rear of his property was a small lake with an Adirondack chair near the shore. Several times a week when the weather was mild, Eric strolled back to the lake, sat in the chair, and watched the birds that frolicked nearby: Canada geese, great blue herons, belted kingfishers, tree swallows, and red-headed woodpeckers. He delighted in cottony clouds drifting by, white sails on a blue ocean. While he saw the birds and the clouds, he did not always look at them intently, for his mind and heart were being pulled toward God. Sitting by the lake soothed his troubled spirit, and eventually he perceived that fluttering birds and majestic clouds were sacraments of God's presence, proof of God's continuing involvement in the world and therefore also in him, Eric.

Contemplation by the lake led to substantive changes. Eric

returned to the Bible with fresh vigor; but now, instead of trying to analyze it, he simply enjoyed it and allowed the words to percolate in him. After a time he also reached out in a new way to his daughter, Susan. They agreed to take turns going to each other's homes for dessert every Sunday afternoon at four o'clock. Despite his grief and continuing dark night, Eric found that he could listen to Susan well enough to help her a little. Out of these conversations Susan tentatively started to date her husband and explore a new relationship, not only for romance but also for honest conversation about their differences.

The day came when Susan and her husband publicly renewed their vows to each other in church on Sunday morning, with their children present. They asked Eric to provide a short meditation, which he did. After the worship service Eric hugged them all—daughter, son-in-law, and grandchildren—and said, "God has been good to you, and good to me too. I am truly blessed." Eric's night ended.

THE DARK NIGHT
IN GROUPS

Do not be afraid, stand firm, and see the deliverance that
the LORD will accomplish for you.

—Exodus 14:13

Many years ago, the Berkey Avenue Mennonite Fellowship in
Goshen, Indiana, entered a dark night. I do not mean that individual members entered their own dark night, although a few of
them may have done so. Instead I mean that the church as a corporate body entered a dark night that affected most, if not all,
of the people who were then attending the congregation.

Apparently the congregation's dark night began when a conflict pushed people into opposing camps and harmed many relationships. When the conflict intensified, some people started leaving for other congregations. The pastor then resigned, believing
that he could no longer work in the congregation. This caused
even more people to leave. One member who decided to stick

with the congregation no matter what said, "So many people were disappearing that when we arrived for worship on Sunday mornings, we looked around anxiously to see who else might have left during the previous week."

Gloom and despair settled over the much smaller congregation that remained. For two years, no one knew what to do, and no aspect of congregational life—worship, education, fellowship, mission, or committee work—was rewarding. Many people were no longer sure how to pray. "It felt that God had forsaken us," said another member.

Then an interim pastor arrived, bringing with him laughter and listening, which proved to be paths out of the dark night. This pastor told lots of jokes, both in person and from the pulpit. He listened patiently to anyone who wanted to talk about the previous two years of impasse, frustration, and abandonment. Through his laughter, people slowly started to laugh again themselves. Through his listening, people slowly learned to trust each other again. Through his gentle presence, people slowly reconnected with the presence of God, which had always been closer to them than their own breath. Once his interim ministry concluded and the congregation hired a new pastor, their corporate life was well on the way to transformation. New people, many of whom had just moved to the area from other parts of the country, arrived and settled into the congregation.

Corporate Dark Nights

So far, we've looked at the dark night in the lives of individual people, but it also occurs in groups in which it becomes a corporate, shared experience of Godforsakenness. If discerning a dark night in the lives of individuals requires caution and prayerful humility, discerning a dark night in corporate life is even more difficult because of the increased complexity of group life. Possible examples of the dark night in groups could include the following situations:

- A congregation discovers that its respected pastor has been sleeping with a sequence of women. The shocking news leaves them feeling that God has betrayed them, which in turn makes it difficult to worship with praise.
- A congregation that was once politically influential and highly popular in town has now declined to fifteen members, all over the age of seventy. Their building, formerly considered an architectural jewel, crumbles around them. Officials in the denomination talk about shutting them down, and the members wonder why God seems to have abandoned them.
- A church institution is forced to lay off a number of employees because of declining income. As the organization seems to lose its way, gloom and foreboding surround those who remain.
- In the wake of a denominational merger, many congregations decide to leave. Those that remain do not yet feel as loyal to the new organizational structures as they were to the ones in the predecessor denominations. Some wonder if God was really in this merger.
- Residents over a widespread area suffer tremendous loss after hurricanes pummel their region. They ask where God was when all this devastation happened.
- During the period of slavery in the United States, significant numbers of African-Americans persistently felt that God had walked away from them as a people.[26]

Israel at the Red Sea

The Israelites passed through a number of experiences that had the flavor of a corporate dark night. One of these occurred on the shore of the Red Sea, just after their escape from Egypt. As night fell, the people of Israel were trapped: ahead of them was an impassable body of water and behind them the swift chariots of Egypt were poised, archers at the ready. With no way to cross the water ahead of them and no hope of defeating one of the world's most fearsome armies behind them, the Israelites felt certain they were about to die. It appeared God had ushered them out of Egypt to let them die in the wilderness.

> As Pharaoh drew near, the Israelites looked back, and there were the Egyptians advancing on them. In great fear the Israelites cried out to the LORD. They said to Moses, "Was it because there were no graves in Egypt that you have taken us away to die in the wilderness? What have you done to us, bringing us out of Egypt? Is this not the very thing we told you in Egypt, 'Let us alone and let us serve the Egyptians'? For it would have been better for us to serve the Egyptians than to die in the wilderness." (Exodus 14:10-12)

Trapped in an Impasse

A mark of the dark night in group life (and in individuals) can be the sense of being trapped in an impasse. We feel stuck in a situation in which we cannot seem to find an effective solution. Solutions that may have worked well in the past no longer do so. We experiment with new approaches to the problem, but they also fail. After exhausting every possibility we can think of, sheer necessity may force us to set aside rational approaches to solving the problem and to look instead for approaches wrapped in mystery, paradox, surprise, or darkness. Biblical faith testifies that paradox and surprise are the very things God specializes in. God often meets us in our impasse, unexpectedly creating a way forward that we could not have imagined.[27]

The impasse of the dark night pushes us toward God and restructures the way we solve problems. That night on the shore of the Red Sea, the Israelites knew they had no solution to the impasse. It seemed God had abandoned them to die in a hopeless, bloody battle against the vastly superior Egyptian army.

A Way Through the Impasse

One of the many benefits of the dark night is that we lean

more heavily on God to see us through difficulties. The lack of options in an impasse pushes us to seek God more persistently, even while we feel that God is gone. Our situation is so desperate that the only hope for newness lies with God. A woman whose family was trapped together in the impasse of a dark night once told me, "We just felt like walking away from God, because it seemed that God had walked away from us. But then there were these moments of desperation when we thought, 'What are we doing? We have to keep walking toward God as best we know how to, because if God doesn't help us, we're all going down the sink.'"

God does offer alternatives to impasse. We may not be able to see these God-given alternatives immediately, and they may not appear as soon as we want them to; yet at the right time, God forges a path through impasse. When all options die, God births new options. During the crisis on the shore of the Red Sea, Moses calmly assured his fellow Israelites that God would soon launch another option that no one has imagined: "Do not be afraid, stand firm, and see the deliverance that the LORD will accomplish for you today; for the Egyptians whom you see today you shall never see again. The LORD will fight for you, and you have only to keep still" (Exodus 14:13-14). Here Moses offered three crucial counsels for people who are in a corporate dark night.

First, do not be afraid. Fear is a natural response to the dark night's impasse. We are scared because we know we are no longer in control. We fear that we've lost God, that we'll die, or that we'll suffer beyond what we can bear. It's not easy to put aside our fear when chaos and impassability threaten to undo us. Yet the admonition not to be afraid frequently appears in the Bible. A foundational characteristic of Christian maturity is trusting God to be good and thereby finding the freedom to set aside our many fears.

Second, stand firm and keep still. The Israelites were tempted to run away from their impasse—even though they didn't know in which direction to run. But Moses knew that running would be foolish because the Egyptians could easily catch them in those swift chariots. So his counsel to stand firm and keep still makes practical sense. In dark nights, we too are tempted to "run" by working harder to solve the problem, by frantically inventing solutions that make little sense, or by blaming ourselves for the mess we're in. But in an impasse, our plans and proposals will likely not help. Standing firm and waiting on God to make a way for us may be the most sensible course of action. Since God uses the dark night to purify us of lesser loves, and since purification rarely happens quickly, the spiritual practice of standing firm and keeping still in loving attentiveness to God is one of the best ways to respond to an impasse.

Third, see the deliverance of God. With this advice Moses invited his fellow Israelites to remember how God had delivered them from the clutches of Egypt just days before. If God saved once, God could certainly save again. God's business, asserted Moses, is to deliver, because saving is intrinsic to God's character. However, God chooses both the time and the means of deliverance, and these rarely match our sense of urgency or our convictions about how the situation should be resolved. I learned a saying many years ago from a friend in the African-American community: "The Spirit don't always come when you want Her, but She always comes on time." We wait in the dark night, living in hope and faith that God's alternative future is at hand (see Mark 1:14-15).

A Path through the Sea

While the Israelites' hearts quaked in terror during the deepest part of the night at the Red Sea, God began the act of deliverance by repositioning the pillar of cloud and fire.

> The angel of God who was going before the Israelite army moved and went behind them; and the pillar of cloud moved from in front of them and took its place behind them. It came between the army of Egypt and the army of Israel. And so the cloud was there with the darkness, and it

lit up the night; one did not come near the other all night.
(Exodus 14:19-20)

With Israel protected from annihilation, God next sent the wind of the Spirit to blow dry a path of deliverance where there had not been a path before. "The LORD drove the sea back by a strong east wind all night, and turned the sea into dry land; and the waters were divided. The Israelites went into the sea on dry ground, the waters forming a wall for them on their right and on their left" (verses 21-22).

Egypt's army galloped after Israel in blind pursuit; but with an impeccable sense of timing, God's wind halted and the sea of water collapsed to destroy the Egyptian military. At this liberation from impasse, Israel's faith in God increased. "Thus the LORD saved Israel that day from the Egyptians; and Israel saw the Egyptians dead on the seashore. Israel saw the great work that the LORD did against the Egyptians. So the people feared the LORD and believed in the LORD and in his servant Moses" (verses 30-31).

The Exile: Another Corporate Dark Night

Hundreds of years after the impasse at the Red Sea, the southern nation of Judah entered another significant corporate dark night. In 586 BC, the Babylonians destroyed Jerusalem and exiled its people to other places in the Ancient Near East, sending a spiritual tsunami through the Jewish people. In the space of a few days, every major institution the Jews had put their faith in was systematically destroyed. According to the final chapter of Jeremiah, the Babylonian military

- blinded the last Jewish king, Zedekiah, and dragged him off in chains to a Babylonian prison (see 52:11);
- broke down the walls around Jerusalem, leaving it defenseless against future attacks (see verse 14);
- removed all worship utensils from inside the temple and carted them off to Babylon (see verses 17-19);

- torched the temple, the king's palace, and all other houses in Jerusalem (see verse 13);
- assassinated key religious, military, and government leaders (see verses 24-27).

After this massive destruction, all three signs of the dark night appeared among the Jewish survivors. First, they could no longer pray in the Jerusalem temple as they had been accustomed to doing. Second, most of life's satisfactions, including adequate food, peace, national security, and various religious practices, were taken away. Third, Jews openly questioned why God allowed all this to happen. Had God suddenly forgotten Israel and dumped her by the wayside? They yearned for God, and yet from all appearances God had disappeared.

This corporate dark night, further expressed in deportation and exile to other parts of the Ancient Near East, caused Jews to rethink their old theology in new and radical ways. A rich variety of Jewish theological voices emerged in the wake of the exile, including the voice of corporate lament.

Launching into Lament

Lament had long been an accepted response to suffering in Jewish faith, but before the exile, it was largely a personal, individual practice, as in Job and in many of the psalms. During the exile, lament became more of a corporate practice precisely because the exile and its resulting night were corporate events. The Jewish people found comfort in corporate lament during the dark night of exile.

The book of Jeremiah ends with a detailed description of massive national destruction. It's no accident that Lamentations, the very next book of the Bible, launches into sustained, intensely emotional lament, for only this kind of lament can match such destruction. Lamentations has five separate poems of lament, one in each chapter. The first four are acrostic poems in which each verse begins with a different letter of the Hebrew alphabet. This poetic structure suggests that the suffering stretches from *aleph* (the first letter of the alphabet) to *taw* (the last letter of the alphabet), or as we might say in English, "Our suffering goes from A to Z."

The opening lines of the first poem grimly survey the widespread physical damage and emotional wreckage in what is left of Jerusalem.

> How lonely sits the city
>   that once was full of people!
> How like a widow she has become,
>   she that was great among the nations!
> She that was a princess among the provinces
>   has become a vassal.
>
> She weeps bitterly in the night,
>   with tears on her cheeks;
> among all her lovers
>   she has no one to comfort her;
> all her friends have dealt treacherously with her,
>   they have become her enemies.
>
> Judah has gone into exile with suffering
>   and hard servitude;
> she lives now among the nations,
>   and finds no resting place;
> her pursuers have all overtaken her
>   in the midst of her distress.
>
> The roads to Zion mourn,
>   for no one comes to the festivals;
> all her gates are desolate,
>   her priests groan;
> her young girls grieve,
>   and her lot is bitter. (Lamentations 1:1-4)

When we enter a dark night, either individually or corporately, we often feel like lamenting. The sense of God's absence is so great, the silence of God so extensive, and the searing agony of psychic suffering so deep that the most spiritually healthy response, as well as the most satisfying one, may be to lament. Israel gave itself permission to express the full range of emotions to God: sometimes Israel could lose itself in praise (for example, Psalms 146–150), while at other times Israel knew that praise was neither possible nor spiritually wise. Intense dark nights are one of the times when lament is better than praise. Since God knows our emotional state anyway, we are free to communicate all our emotions to God, including the emotions of lament.

Nearly every worship service in the North American church is organized around praise, especially in the songs and prayers. Lament in our worship is rare indeed. I grew up in a relatively poor congregation in an obviously poor neighborhood where people had plenty of things to lament about; yet the worship services oddly, and unfailingly, focused on praise. The closest some worship services come to lament may be the sharing of joys and concerns, when I've often witnessed people weep as they ask others to pray for a friend or family member who is extremely ill. Lamenting about medical issues happens commonly enough, but I recall only a few instances when people lamented about losing a job, declaring bankruptcy, failing to find vocational fulfillment, or some other disaster. Once, I helped to plan a special worship service for victims of domestic violence. There was plenty of individual and corporate lament in that service, and it was one of the most meaningful, gut-wrenchingly real worship services I've ever been in. Our faith might become deeper and richer if we allowed ourselves to lament more than we do.

Biblical lament does not mince words but bluntly tells it like it is. The act of lamenting is so physically visceral that it taxes the human body.

My eyes are spent with weeping;
    my stomach churns;
my bile is poured out on the ground
    because of the destruction of my people,
because infants and babes faint
    in the streets of the city. (Lamentations 2:11)

Look at Us!

Lamentations pleads with God to remember the terrible desolation that has happened and to look at and pay attention to the people's dark night.

Remember, O LORD, what has befallen us;
    look, and see our disgrace! (5:1)

After this general plea to "look, and see," the poet lists specific sufferings in and around Jerusalem that God should notice. The person almost hurls them into God's face.

Our inheritance has been turned over to strangers,
    our homes to aliens.
We have become orphans, fatherless;
    our mothers are like widows.
We must pay for the water we drink;
    the wood we get must be bought.
With a yoke on our necks we are hard driven;
    we are weary, we are given no rest. . . .
Slaves rule over us;
    there is no one to deliver us from their hand.
We get our bread at the peril of our lives,
    because of the sword in the wilderness.
Our skin is black as an oven
    from the scorching heat of famine.
Women are raped in Zion,
    virgins in the towns of Judah.
Princes are hung up by their hands;
    no respect is shown to the elders.
Young men are compelled to grind,

and boys stagger under loads of wood.
The old men have left the city gate,
     the young men their music.
The joy of our hearts has ceased;
     our dancing has been turned to mourning. (5:2-5, 8-15)

When God does not respond, the poet accuses God of hiding in a dark, impenetrable night, of abandoning Israel and refusing to communicate.

You have wrapped yourself with a cloud
     so that no prayer can pass through. . . .
Why have you forgotten us completely?
     Why have you forsaken us these many days? (3:44; 5:20)

A Reply of Silence

God remained silent throughout Lamentations, never saying anything and never responding to Israel's pleas. While the book is full of human speech, divine speech is absent. Lamentations therefore ends with a poignant plea from people whose life is on the edge. In the final prayer, people plead for the restoration of intimacy with God. Yet because God remains shrouded in darkness and silence, they must consider the frightful possibility that God will never again have anything to do with them.

Restore us to yourself, O LORD, that we may be restored;
     renew our days as of old—
unless you have utterly rejected us,
     and are angry with us beyond measure. (5:21-22)

Lamentations, and the experience of exile from which it comes, functions in the Old Testament a bit like Jesus' crucifixion functions in the New Testament. Both are pivotal moments when hope appears to have ended and the future seems to hold only extreme hardship and deep despair. In the depths of lament, praise is nearly impossible and hope is thin. Yet the book of Lamentations is not the last word—either in the Bible itself or in our experience as God's people—just as Jesus' crucifixion is not the last word. What appears to be an impasse is but a prelude to unimagined new life. Something wonderful always lies on the other side of the dark night: not only purification and renewal but also a new relationship with God.

Effects of a Corporate Dark Night

When a group of people emerges from a dark night, its goals will often be clearer, its mission more refined, and its vision more compelling. As lament passes, people in the congregation, agency, or institution usually are energized to collaborate with each other in fresh ways. Some of the most fruitful years in a group's history frequently follow a dark night. People itch to find ways of expressing their gratitude and service to God. They persistently seek a new or newly focused mission through which they can witness to a magnificent God.

During and after the exile, this happened among Jews, who developed new ways of being Jewish that did not rely on having a temple and a king in Jerusalem. For example, they became a people of the book. The Jewish scriptures (our Old Testament) were collected, shaped, and edited into their final form. Study of these scriptures then became a central focus of Jewish life. Instead of priests who offered sacrifices, rabbis became the most important leaders, in no small part because they devoted themselves to the study and interpretation of scripture. Instead of having one centrally located temple in Jerusalem, Jews congregated into small, local synagogues that they could take with them anywhere in the world. With these three new forms of religious life—scripture, rabbi, and synagogue—Jews have adapted remarkably well over the centuries in many different cultures and political settings. Despite periodic persecution, they have managed to retain their unique identity and sense of peoplehood. In important ways the dark night of their Babylonian exile resulted in significant gifts that have sustained Jewish people for many centuries.

Renewed Congregational Life

This chapter began with the story of a dark night that swept through Berkey Avenue Mennonite Fellowship, the congregation where I am now a pastor. Long before I arrived in 2002, the congregation experienced renewal in the wake of its dark night.

The renewal began with an interim pastor who helped the congregation to laugh and listen. The emphasis on healing frayed relationships continued with the arrival of a new, long-term pastor. Soon an assortment of younger families moved in, settled down, and invested themselves in congregational life. At about this time, the congregation also purchased new hymnals that reinvigorated worship with a selection of fresh music.

As optimism expanded, the members developed a new vision statement that emphasized intimacy and invitation as core values. A motto, "Called to be Christ's loving, healing, caring presence," spontaneously arose from within congregational life. A group within the church began hosting homeless people in the church building, taking turns with half a dozen other congregations in town that also hosted in their buildings.

Eventually numerical growth was strong enough to require a second pastor. For the first time in its history, the congregation hired a woman, giving the pastoral team a set of skills and sensibilities that further enhanced vitality. Because of a dark night, God worked through the congregation to renew relationships, refine purpose, and expand mission.

Part 4

THE NIGHT'S CONVERSIONS

—11—

FAITH IN THE FACE
OF SUFFERING

We are afflicted in every way, but not crushed; perplexed,
but not driven to despair; persecuted, but not forsaken;
struck down, but not destroyed; always carrying in the
body the death of Jesus, so that the life of Jesus may also
be made visible in our bodies.

—2 Corinthians 4:8-10

Now faith is the assurance of things hoped for, the conviction of things not seen.

—Hebrews 11:1

The second section of this book explored how the dark night
affects our inner life of prayer, whereas the third section explored
the night's appearances in our vocations, families, and groups.
This fourth and final section focuses on some of the dark night's
conversions. How does the night change us over the long term?
What lasting results does God create in us via the night?

169

The night can birth at least three results: our faith deepens in the face of suffering, our relationship with God changes into an intimate friendship, and our life in the world takes on the character of countercultural mission. We take a chapter for each of these conversions, beginning here in this chapter by focusing on how God's actions in the dark night, amid significant suffering, forge in us a deeper faith.

Dark nights have varying levels of suffering. Some nights are relatively mild and others intense. The same dark night can also vary in intensity while running its course. It can start lightly and become increasingly heavy, or begin with a bang and end with a whimper. It can start small, balloon up in the middle, and deflate again at the end. Or it might begin in concentrated form, dilute as it ages, and then get thicker again before it finally dissolves and fades away. The intensity can increase or decrease week by week, even day by day. The Spirit adjusts the levels of intensity depending on what needs to be purified in us and on how well we are able to tolerate the process of purification. We begin with the story of Heather.

Heather

Forty-nine-year-old Heather was the pastor of Plum Ridge Church, a congregation of 135 people in rural Colorado. From the beginning of her pastorate six years ago, Plum Ridge grew by about twenty people. Although she was not an imaginative preacher, she was an able administrator, a clear thinker, and a compassionate caregiver. The congregation responded well to her leadership, so much so that the initial honeymoon between her and the members had not yet ended.

The cream on all this was her relationship with God. During her first six years at Plum Ridge, Heather and God were intimate, at least as far as Heather could tell. Sure, her relationship with God went up and down, sometimes feeling closer than at other times, but overall it was warm enough that she usually felt some kind of meaningful connection with God. A big part of her spirituality was experiencing God through creation. One of her favorite places to pray was in the living room of the parsonage, with its three large windows looking out onto the Colorado Rockies. Another favorite spot was the prayer garden she created in the back yard, which had a comfortable bench in front of a pool and fountain, surrounded by native flowers, bushes, and grasses. Since moving to Colorado, Heather's favorite passages of Scripture had been Psalms 65 and 104, both fervent expressions of praise to God for the created world.

> By your strength you established the mountains;
>   you are girded with might. . . .
> Those who live at earth's farthest bounds are awed by your signs;
>   you make the gateways of the morning and the evening
>   shout for joy. (Psalm 65:6, 8)

Heather, in other words, thought of herself as a relatively successful pastor—until halfway through her sixth year at Plum Ridge, when she was plunged into a cavernous dark night. Outwardly her relationships with members of the congregation remained affectionate, and from the congregation's point of view, Heather was still as effective and industrious as ever.

But inwardly she fell into a crisis of faith unlike anything she had known before. It seemed that God had disappeared. She wanted to believe that God was still God and that God continued to work in the lives of her congregants. But she could not bring herself to believe it. When she stood behind the pulpit on Sundays to preach, pray, and lead worship, she felt like a robot, mouthing the words but having no more soul than a Pentium processor running a giant but mostly empty hard drive, whirling without purpose.

At home she was habitually irritable. At church her relationships with people in the congregation felt as though they had no direction. "Why do we work so hard at trying to be the church?" she wondered to herself. "Is all this frenetic activity really worth it—the committees, the potluck meals, the ceaseless stream of announcements, the fundraising, the hospital visits, the endless cycle of Advent and Christmas and then of Lent and Easter, and all the other busyness of church life? What does any of this have to do with God?"

In her personal life, Heather could no longer pray with conviction. In fact, she could not pray with words at all. The view of the Rocky Mountains from her living room windows remained as grand as ever, but it no longer made her heart sing. Her prayer paradise in the back yard might as well have been a vast, empty desert, though she frequently sat there in silence and solitude, wanting to connect with God. When she cracked her Bible, it naturally opened to the pages containing Psalms 65 and 104, but she could not stand to read from either psalm. Instead she turned to Job, finding peevish solace in its complaint about God's absence.

> "Today also my complaint is bitter;
>   his hand is heavy despite my groaning.
> Oh, that I knew where I might find him,
>   that I might come even to his dwelling!
> I would lay my case before him,
>   and fill my mouth with arguments.
> I would learn what he would answer me,
>   and understand what he would say to me. . . .
> [But] if I go forward, he is not there;
>   or backward, I cannot perceive him;
> on the left he hides, and I cannot behold him;
>   I turn to the right, but I cannot see him." (23:2-5, 8-9)

After several months of wandering around listlessly in the book of Job, she found her way back to the Psalms. By now she was furious with God for leaving her. One afternoon she stood in her yard facing the mountains, and using the words of the psalmist, yelled at the top of her voice.

> Rouse yourself! Why do you sleep, O Lord?
>   Awake, do not cast us off forever!
> Why do you hide your face? (44:23-24)

After nearly a year of being angry with God, Heather settled into frigidity. The image that came to her was of being all alone in the Antarctic, walking aimlessly in a blinding snowstorm, seeing nothing but driving snow, hearing nothing but howling wind, feeling nothing but bitter cold. She wanted God badly, yet God seemed to care nothing for her. The Scripture that now meant the most to her was the one Jesus uttered from the cross.

> My God, my God, why have you forsaken me?
>> Why are you so far from helping me, from the words of my groaning?
> O my God, I cry by day, but you do not answer;
>> and by night, but find no rest. (22:1-2)

Heather felt like "groaning" because she increasingly saw her own sinfulness, particularly the sin of envy. Envy was not new sin for her, but rather old sin that had been lurking in the shadows of her life for many years. She now realized how much she envied Grace Community Church, a visibly successful congregation in a nearby town: its 320 members, its new building and flashy programs, and its Sunday-morning radio broadcast on a local radio station. In particular she envied the lead pastor, who was regarded as an insightful preacher. Her new awareness of persistent envy often led her to whisper several times throughout the day, "Have mercy on me, O God, . . . for I know my transgressions, and my sin is ever before me" (Psalm 51:1, 3).

Heather's dark night lasted eleven years, taking umpteen twists and turns. Her inner suffering was so intense that at various points along the way she almost resigned from the pastorate and left Christian faith altogether. Had it not been for the sympathy and support of her husband, Tim, she might have done just that. But she neither resigned nor left Christ.

As the night continued, she slowly came to realize that she was being spiritually purged in a deep and thorough way. She saw that she had been obsessively attached to the dream of success, to her self-image as a competent person, to her unusual ability to develop caring relationships, and to the honeymoon of the first six years at Plum Ridge. She realized she had allowed these attachments to become hungry gods that demanded more and more of her soul that was meant to worship Yahweh alone.

Most of all, she perceived that her former faith in God was being dismantled to make way for a new, more radical kind of faith. She was being stripped of the assumption that her emotional state accurately measured the presence or absence of God. She was being deprived of the belief that vocational success proved God was blessing her. She was learning that Christian discipleship sometimes means sheer dogged perseverance, that Jesus sometimes asks you to follow him through the intense suffering of emotional emptiness, intellectual obscurity, and spiritual deprivation.

One day near the end of her eleven-year ordeal, Heather was reading the Gospel of Matthew and was captured in a new way by one of Jesus' shorter parables: "Again, the kingdom of heaven is like a merchant in search of fine pearls; on finding one pearl of great value, he went and sold all that he had and bought it" (13:45-46).

She walked over to her desk, found her journal and a pen, and sat down to write:

> This parable describes what's happened to me over the last decade. I'm the merchant, except that I didn't choose to go out and sell the pearls of my old faith so that I could buy this "one pearl of great value." God made me sell those old, inferior pearls. God took them away, and I kicked and screamed most of the time. But looking back, I now see what I couldn't see at the time: that God did this for my own good, that the pearls I thought were so precious—my hope for numerical and programmatic success, my reputation in the community, my emotional highs that at the time felt so "spiritual," my thin faith—that all of these were in fact cheap costume jewelry.

The other thing I now see is that hidden deep in the soil of my life was a far more beautiful pearl that I did not create or give to myself. This flawless pearl came as a gift from God and is beyond anything I could think or imagine. I cannot put a price on its value because no money on earth could buy it. It came to me after intense suffering that I did not ask for and would not want to go through again. Yet now that God has given me such a luminous pearl, I would not trade it for anything. This pearl of faith glows with the light of Christ. It impels me to radical service—not for my glory, but for the glory of Jesus Christ.

During her dark night, Heather was afflicted but not crushed, perplexed but not quite driven to complete despair (see 2 Corinthians 4:8).

Suffering

Suffering comes in many forms. Sometimes the dark night arises from profound outward suffering that other people can see, such as debilitating illness, public humiliation, the death of a close friend, or dozens of other afflictions that life throws at us. One of the questions I am often asked is whether God brings about the many forms of outward suffering that we human beings experience. Does God cause hurricanes, cancer, war, or traffic accidents? No, I do not think so. These things happen because of how the natural world sometimes functions (hurricanes), because of the way our bodies sometimes malfunction (cancer), because of human greed and lust for power (war), or because of human error and misjudgment (traffic accidents). God does not cause these types of outward suffering. When these events happen, God remains with us, offering us comfort and hope even while we suffer.

However, God *might* use these external sufferings as an opportunity to lead us inwardly into a dark night that purifies us and furthers the development of contemplation, or God *might not* use them to initiate a dark night. Sometimes our outward suffering will lead to a dark night, while at other times it will not. Another way to say this is that not every form of suffering is a dark night, but every dark night involves some form of suffering.

The suffering of a dark night might be purely internal. This was true for Heather, whose night came while she was outwardly successful and had no significant external suffering. In cases like hers, suffering comes from the dark night itself and will remain largely internal and therefore beyond what most people can notice, even some of our friends. Our suffering comes precisely because it seems that God no longer cares for us. We feel bereft and desperate. We find no relief. For a while we may feel that we and God are opponents. We wonder if we will ever experience God's love again.

Because it feels like God is not being the sort of kind, gentle, and loving God that we thought we were serving, our suffering can make us bitter. "Is this the way you treat your followers?" we might say to God. "What did I do to deserve this abandonment? True, sometimes I didn't do what I should have, and other times I deliberately did what I shouldn't have. But all in all, I'm not such a bad person! I go to church and put my tithe in the offering. I've never committed adultery or killed anyone. I even drive the speed limit. And now you leave me? How am I supposed to trust in your love and goodness? What kind of God are you?"

In this situation very little comforts us for long. Instead we are invited to walk through the valley of dogged perseverance. Will we maintain our commitment to Christ, even when there are no rewards? Will we persist in the journey of faith even when we see no light ahead? Stripped of the spiritual comforts and assurances that once sustained us, will we allow pure faith to carry us forward?

The Gift of Pure Faith

Heather's dark night was longer and more intense than most. After eleven years of sticking with a God she could not sense, feel, or imagine in satisfying ways, she began to emerge from the valley of dogged perseverance, her fidelity to God strengthened. Early in the dark night she thought she had lost God. Only near the end of her trial did she discover that what she really lost were her false illusions about God. She found out that God does not sit in heaven doling out candy but guides us through the valley of suffering to the pearl of inestimable worth.

This pearl is pure faith. Through the suffering of the dark night, we eventually come to a place of sheer faith, stripped to its bare knuckles. We learn that in all of heaven and earth, we have nothing and no one but God, because everything else is taken away from us: our false self-image, our vaporous dreams, our petty preoccupations. We learn that even if God seems to forsake us (which God never does), we have no one else to turn to except God. We learn that God is our all.

As we emerge from the night we discover that we have been given a fabulous gift: we can now trust God in spite of all evidence to the contrary. Our new trust is not so much a trust in God's promises, but trust in God as a person. In a newly authentic way, we trust God in the marrow of our bones. With this trust woven into the fiber of our being, we no longer need to understand everything about Christian faith. We can handle mystery, spiritual paradox, and further trials without them stealing our trust in the fidelity of God.

Temptations

We do not come to this pearl of pure trust easily, because the temptations to flee the path of darkness are powerful. Our chief temptation is to chase after other things that we hope will fill our darkness—to find something, anything, that will make us feel good for a brief moment. We might go on a shopping spree in a misguided attempt to make ourselves feel better. We might be tempted to indulge in a sexual affair as a foolish way of giving ourselves fleeting but false moments of pleasure.

I tried several ways of fleeing my deepest darkness. One was gourmet cooking. I bought new cookbooks, new kitchen gadgets, and new ingredients. The large city I was living in at the time gave me many different ethnic food shops to choose from, including Mediterranean, Italian, Indian, Mexican, and Korean. I sampled prosciutto, fresh water buffalo mozzarella, and different varieties of feta cheese. I bought pasta in fancy shapes. One day I nearly bought an ostrich egg (at twelve dollars) to make an ostrich omelet. I learned to make *boeuf bourguignonne* and chocolate mousse. I indulged my lifelong love for cream and butter. The main thing I gained from this intense search for gastronomic satisfaction was twenty pounds around my middle, which I had to take off later through disciplined abstinence. I learned that this search for pleasure was nothing but "chasing after wind" (Ecclesiastes 2:11).

I also tried home improvement projects. I laid new ceramic tile in the bathrooms. I purchased a router to make my own wood molding. I bought strong chemicals to strip the paint from the oak trim in our turn-of-the-century home, searching for the satisfaction of surrounding myself with lovely oak wood. I spackled and repainted walls so they would look pristine. I taught myself special painting effects, such as combing and rag rolling. I changed the color schemes in whole rooms, sometimes more than once. The pleasure I sucked out of doing all these things lasted only a few months before I went on yet another hunt for some new but ultimately shallow aesthetic fix.

During an intense dark night, God prevents us from finding lasting pleasure in anything that is not God. Our central pain here is not receiving the satisfaction, consolation, delight, or rewards we want. After these satisfactions are taken away, we are left with a huge hole at the center of our life that looks bottomless when we stand on the edge of it and peer down. We rightly suspect that only God can fill this hole, and yet to our frustration God seems nowhere to be found. God wants us to stay with this hole, however, because it leads to our healing. Our pain is an inner dying that in due course brings us to the fullness of God's love. Our suffering is not the end of the path. As we cling to the promise that God will care for us, our faith is purified. We believe that God holds us with light and love, even though we neither see it nor feel it. We discover that our feelings do not reliably indicate the presence or absence of God.

It takes time for stronger faith to emerge from suffering. The Spirit wants us to live for a while with the night's inner suffering and to trust that a new expression of God's salvation will grow from it. Living through suffering is one of the things Jesus means by taking up our cross and following him. In brief moments along the way, the new and deeper faith that is unfolding will become visible for a little while, giving us hope that our night might be coming to an end. Then suddenly our newly emerging faith seems to vanish, leaving us extremely discouraged. This up-and-down nature of the dark night is common. Yet each time the up-and-down cycle happens, our faith grows a little stronger and stays visible a little longer. As the purification of the night concludes, our new, deeper faith will prevail to become a permanent fixture of our spiritual life.

We make a deeper decision to commit ourselves completely to God during this intense night, to follow Jesus without reservation, and to open ourselves wholly to the Spirit. Earlier in life our commitment to Christ was partial, made with a closed fist that held something back. While we wanted to commit ourselves to God, we also held on to our attachments. Thanks to the purifying work of the Spirit in the dark night, at least some of those attachments are now released. Our hands are more open to receive the new spirit that God wishes to offer us in love.

Testing in the Wilderness

Our faith is tested during the night, a bit like Jesus' faith was tested in the wilderness: "Jesus, full of the Holy Spirit, returned from the Jordan and was led by the Spirit in the wilderness, where for forty days he was tempted by the devil" (Luke 4:1-2).

Often we call these forty wilderness days the "temptation" of Jesus. The Greek word *peirazo* can certainly mean "tempted," but it can also mean "tested." Clearly the devil is tempting Jesus (see Matthew 4:1-11; Luke 4:1-13), yet those temptations also test Jesus in the sense that they help him clarify what his mission will and will not be. They purify his understanding of mission and prepare him for a public ministry that will ultimately take him to the cross. Few of us will live in a physical wilderness for forty days; but if we enter a dark night, we will be tested in a way that similarly clarifies our sense of mission and leads us to countercultural ministry in the world (a subject we will explore further in chapter 13). Intense dark nights, then, are somewhat like the wilderness experience of Jesus. We will be tempted by distractions, but those very temptations test—and strengthen—our faith.

A Shifting Sense of Sinfulness

In the early years after our baptism, we are typically aware of our specific sins. We feel remorse after viewing pornography on the internet, after shopping on the Sabbath, or after giving the cold shoulder to someone at work. We feel guilty when the police cruiser in our rearview mirror, its lights flashing, signals us to pull off the road for driving too fast. At night we cry to God for mercy when we remember the vicious, cutting remark we made to our best friend or to our spouse earlier in the day. If we feel guilty after committing specific sins, it proves that our inner moral compass is still working. Our conscience is alive and well.

In a dark night, particularly an intense one, the awareness of our sin expands. In addition to noticing the specific sins we've committed, we recognize within ourselves a pervasive state of sin bigger than any individual sins. Instead of feeling sorry only for the three or four sins we know we committed today, we also feel guilty for an underlying sense that most of our life, not just little parts of it, is at odds with God. We begin to realize that sin is not simply a series of rebellious acts against God and neighbor; it is also a state of being in which the very structure of our life is out of alignment with God. During the dark night we see *sin*, not simply *sins*.

This doesn't mean we no longer recognize specific sins. To the contrary, we probably notice more specific sins in our life than ever before. Why? Because the dark night is fundamentally about receiving the light of God in a new way. As God's light shines in us during the night, it spotlights sins that until now have remained hidden in the shadows. The specific sins may vary from person to person, but will generally be one or more of the sins that Christians have long recognized: envy, lust, gluttony, anger, sloth, greed, pride, injustice, and murder. God cannot very well help us to get rid of sin if we don't even know the sin is there. So in the night, God aims a bright light at the sin we have successfully managed to hide from ourselves for a long time, even though God has seen that sin since the day it was born. In this divine light we see our sin as it is, without hiding it, denying it, or making excuses for it. Using an intense, focused laser, God then burns up that sin, cauterizes the wound, and nurses us back to better spiritual health.

During and after a dark night, we also perceive the sins of the world more clearly. As I write these words, the wars that the United States began against Afghanistan in 2001 and Iraq in 2003 continue in quagmires. During my lifetime, the United States has fought the Vietnam War, the Cold War with its nuclear arms race, the first Persian Gulf War, and numerous smaller conflicts. Because I am convinced that following Jesus authentically requires nonviolence (see Matthew 5:9, 38-48), I have always felt it to be a great evil whenever the country I live in goes to war. But never before have I felt the evil so deeply in my bones as I have while these wars rage in Afghanistan and Iraq. They may not be any more sinful than previous wars the United States has fought, but something inside me has changed. Because of the dark nights I've been through, I seem to be more sensitive to the sin of war.

The more acute awareness of sin that we experience in the

dark night is itself a form of suffering. Dark nights are painful partly because sin—ours and the world's—is suddenly more visible to us. The sight of sin is ugly and gut wrenching. Newly enabled to see sin as it really is, we realize more fully how sin binds us in its web.

One summer a honeybee flew into an abandoned spider web outside the window of my study. I watched the bee struggle to free itself; but the more it struggled, the more tightly its body and wings became trapped in the threads of the web. A few days later I noticed that the honeybee had died from exhaustion and lack of nutrition.

Sin can similarly trap us. We may struggle mightily against it, but sometimes we cannot break free, just as that honeybee could not. The struggle binds us more tightly into the sin, and unless a greater power intervenes, that sin can kill us. Of course we do have a higher power—God—who can and does intervene to free us from the entanglements of our sin. The dark night is one of God's gracious interventions that cuts the sticky web wrapped around us.

From a practical and pastoral point of view, this means that people in the dark night often feel a compelling need to confess their sin regularly in order to receive God's forgiveness. In my work as a pastor, I've noticed two groups of people who particularly crave opportunities to confess their sin and receive forgiveness. The first group consists of people who've just been caught in an obvious, humiliating sin like adultery, murder, or financial cheating. The second group consists of people in the dark night. People in this second group often yearn for weekly, even daily confession. Congregations that include a confession of sin and pronouncement of forgiveness in each week's worship service offer a tremendous gift to people in the dark night.

Yearning to Die and Be with Christ

In extreme cases of the dark night, we might wish for our own death in order to be closer to God. By itself the wish for death is not necessarily morbid. Paul himself wished for death in his letter to the Philippians as he sat in prison and awaited trial before the Roman emperor. Paul knew that at the end of the trial the emperor could sentence him to death. While we can't be sure, the emperor actually may have sentenced Paul to die at this trial, resulting in Paul's death shortly afterward. Whatever happened, Paul clearly welcomed the possibility of dying, because he could then "depart and be with Christ, for that is far better" (Philippians 1:23).

This yearning for death during a dark night is not macabre, spooky, or weird, but a perfectly normal result of our growing friendship with Christ. (For more on friendship, see the next chapter.) We are willing to die because we want to experience more intimacy with Christ (see again Philippians 1:23). Let me be clear and say that this is not the same thing as wishing for or making plans to commit suicide. Looking forward to death is simply a yearning to be intimate once again with God—an intimacy that for now we cannot feel. Our suffering over God's perceived absence makes us look forward to leaving this life and being with Christ, our all in all. Wishing, of course, does not mean we immediately get what we want. We cannot choose the hour of our own death, but have to wait for it to come at some unknown point in the future. This waiting can be yet another instance of our suffering during the night.

What Tim Saw

One of the night's conversions, then, is the transformation of our faith. How did this play out for Heather?

When we left her earlier in this chapter, Heather had just finished writing a journal entry on the parable of the pearl of great price. Over the next few years, her husband, Tim, noticed a number of changes in her. First, he noticed that Heather no longer worried about what would happen to her when she died; she appeared to be confident that God would receive her into eternal life. Second, he realized that she had a far deeper capacity to wait peacefully with other people who were suffering, even in situations in which it seemed that the suffering had no end in this life. Third, he witnessed in her an overriding desire to do the right thing, regardless of how it might affect her reputation. And fourth, he detected in her the flowering of a new relationship with God. When he shared this last observation with her, Heather replied, "Yes, the way I would put it is that God has now become my friend."

This friendship with God is another conversion the dark night creates—our subject for the next chapter.

NEW FRIENDSHIP WITH GOD AND CREATION

I do not call you servants any longer, because the servant does not know what the master is doing; but I have called you friends, because I have made known to you everything that I have heard from my Father.

—John 15:15

As the suffering of the dark night passes and the gold of our faith is purified of its dross, we receive the great gift of a new friendship with God. In 2005 I interviewed fifteen people about their experience of the dark night. I wanted to find out how the dark night had changed them or, if they were still in a dark night, how it was changing them. To my surprise, almost all of them (fourteen out of fifteen) spoke about a new, growing sense of friendship with God. The only person who did not speak of this seemed to have been in a relatively early stage of the dark night and did not yet know what new image of God was being formed in her. She knew that the dark night was dismantling her old images of God, but she could not yet describe what was being formed in her, even though she sensed that something new was ready to be born. I would not be surprised if eventually she also came to see God as a friend. To understand how the dark night births this new friendship, I begin with the story of Joe.

From Judge to Friend

Joe grew up in a tightly knit network of Christians in a small town where God was portrayed as stern, scary, and demanding. "At dinner time," Joe remembered, "my father would bow his head and almost always begin his prayer with the words 'O righteous, fearsome, omnipotent Lord, we lower our faces in awe at your great majesty and ever-watchful eye.'" Joe heard similar words from the pulpit on Sundays. "On the day of my baptism at the age of fifteen," he said, "the pastor used the opening lines of Psalm 38, changing the pronouns from 'me' and 'mine' to 'us' and 'ours'—and of course all this was in the old King James Version."

> O Lord, rebuke us not in thy wrath:
>> neither chasten us in thy hot displeasure.
> For thine arrows stick fast in us,
>> and thy hand presseth us sore.
> There is no soundness in our flesh because of thine anger;
>> neither is there any rest in our bones because of our sin.
> For our iniquities are gone over our heads:
>> as a heavy burden they are too heavy for us.
> Our wounds stink and are corrupt
>> because of our foolishness.
> We are troubled; we are bowed down greatly;
>> we go mourning all the day long.
> For our loins are filled with a loathsome disease:
>> and there is no soundness in our flesh.
> (Psalm 38:1-7, adapted from the KJV)

As a consequence of the severe religion of his childhood, Joe entered adulthood afraid of God. "Deep down," he said, "I felt that God probably hated me, even though I was baptized, went to church, and did all the right things. In truth, I had a pretty low self-image."

At age twenty-seven, Joe entered a dark night. It began after his employer, one of the big three auto manufacturers, laid off seventeen thousand workers because of declining sales. Joe, who worked at a plant that made SUVs, was included in the layoff. While the layoff did not completely surprise him, it was deeply discouraging nonetheless. After that he could not pray or worship with enthusiasm. Why did God allow this to happen to him? When Joe went to talk to his pastor about it, his pastor told him to pray harder. But how was he supposed to do that when petitionary prayer, his usual way of praying, was as dead as a socket wrench? How was prayer possible when heaven seemed to have no God in it?

During the months he was out of work, Joe thumbed through the Scriptures, searching for passages that would help him understand why God seemed distant. Most Scripture had little or no meaning for him, but he did find a few passages he had never paid much attention to before. One of these became his favorite, maybe because Joe himself sometimes went fishing and could imagine what it was like to get caught on a lake during a storm.

> When evening came, his disciples went down to the sea, got into a boat, and started across the sea to Capernaum. It was now dark. . . . The sea became rough because a strong wind was blowing. When they had rowed about three or four miles, they saw Jesus walking on the sea and coming near the boat, and they were terrified. But he said to them, "It is I; do not be afraid." (John 6:16-20)

He read the passage in different translations until it became so vivid in his mind that he could almost hear the wind howling, see the waves bouncing the boat, and feel the terror of being trapped on open water. But what meant the most to him was imagining Jesus walking on the water toward the boat, assuring the disciples that they did not have to be afraid of him. "My image of God started to change with that passage," said Joe. "It was a different picture of God than the one I grew up with—not scary, but caring and gentle. I began to see in my head that God could love me and care for me. God wasn't there to watch every bad move I made, and then at the slightest infraction of the rules, toss me into hell."

Joe and his wife eventually moved to another town, where he found work at a tool-and-die plant. In that town they found a new church that offered an adult Sunday-school class on contemplative prayer. Although Joe had never heard of contemplative prayer, he agreed to attend the class when a fellow employee from the plant, who was also a member of the church, invited him. Joe figured that if his old ways of praying weren't working anyway, why not experiment with something different?

One Sunday the teacher brought a portable labyrinth to class, spread it out on the floor, explained what it was and how to do it, and then invited the rest of the class to join her in walking. Though he was skeptical, Joe decided to be a good sport and see what would happen. By the time he walked out of the labyrinth he realized something had happened to him. He felt a new connection with God that he hadn't felt in a long time. He felt more light-hearted, almost as if God was breathing in him.

Walking the labyrinth eventually became one of Joe's favorite ways to pray. Many times he imagined Jesus walking with him through the labyrinth, sometimes ahead of him and sometimes beside him. As his dark night dissipated, he sensed that God was not distant but near, not vengeful but loving, not waiting to spring a trap on him but waiting for him to come home. God became a close friend.

Friendship

The dark night changes the way we think of God. Like Joe, some of us imagine God as a demanding tyrant we cannot satisfy, no matter how hard we try. Some of us suppose that if we believe all the right things and do all the right things, God owes us prosperity and perfect health. We think if we tell God what we want and believe it hard enough, we'll automatically get whatever we ask for. Or we expect God to make our life easy by magically fixing a situation that vexes us.

These and other inadequate images of God rarely survive a dark night. Our sense of God's absence crumbles incomplete ideas of God for the simple reason that those ideas no longer make sense to us. The night purifies our attachment to possessions, illusions, practices, feelings, and skewed images of God. During some of the night, we might wonder if we have any images of God left to rely on. By taking away the meaning we formerly found in our God images, God dismantles the box we built to contain who we thought God supposedly is and how God supposedly acts. We discover that God is beyond our container.

This loss of images can be painful—and also exciting. The painful part comes as God strips away our insufficient images to prepare us for receiving new, more complete images of God's character and mission. The exciting part comes as God gives us the gift of contemplation and we experience a new, delightful side of God. This new side of God is wonderfully intimate, warm, gentle, loving, gracious, and peaceful.

As contemplation flowers, we realize that God is as close as our breathing. Prayer no longer happens only at our initiative, but now also happens at God's initiative. It becomes the primary mode of communication between God and us, where we both give and receive. Prayer is like an intimate sharing between friends.[28] Moreover, we recognize that prayer is not limited to mealtimes, bedtimes, and Sunday-morning worship, but can happen at any moment of the day or night, even on the fly while we're doing other things. God's constant, loving activity becomes more visible to us. We learn that praying is not "saying our prayers" as much as simply being open to God, being aware of God, and being responsive to God. Prayer is a way of thinking, feeling, and living continually in response to God.

This does not mean that we quit all forms of focused, intentional prayer. An overly busy lifestyle is deadly to prayer, and we must still set aside certain periods of the day as holy and dedicated exclusively for praying. I've struggled most of my life to find enough time to pray; the responsibilities of marriage, parenting, schooling, and job have often shoved prayer to the margins of my life. Since my most recent dark night, however, prayer has moved from the margin to the center. More than before, I look forward to my two designated times of prayer each day, when I can spend time with my best friend. I want to be with God.

When prayer becomes an intimate sharing between friends, a new peace comes over us. We trust God at a deeper level. We are more united with God's vision for the world, purposes in the world, and power to accomplish what God wants to accomplish in the world. We now live the words of Jesus, "Abide in me as I abide in you. Just as the branch cannot bear fruit by itself unless it abides in the vine, neither can you unless you abide in me. . . . As the Father has loved me, so I have loved you; abide in my love" (John 15:4, 9).

Friendship in Scripture

One of the Bible's most daring images for God is that of a friend. Abraham seems to have been the earliest person to be called God's friend (see 2 Chronicles 20:7; Isaiah 41:8; James 2:23), but others were as well. One of these was Moses, who regularly entered the tent of meeting (or tabernacle) to consult with God about important matters. The cloud of God's presence would descend at the entrance of the tent, where the two of them could then speak freely. Their relationship was intimate. "Thus the LORD used to speak to Moses face to face, as one speaks to a friend" (Exodus 33:11).

In John 15:15, quoted at the beginning of this chapter,

Jesus announced that we are his friends. We are not his "slaves" (the more accurate meaning of the Greek word *doulous*, which the NRSV translates as "servants"), who mindlessly follow his orders without understanding his plans and purposes. Instead we are Jesus' friends, who know his mind because we have an intimate relationship with him. Our friendship with Jesus begins at our baptism and grows as we engage in the practices of worship, study, prayer, and service. For many people, the dark night pushes this friendship with Christ to new heights so that Jesus virtually becomes our constant companion.

Luke deftly illustrates this friendship in his story about the two disciples who walked back home to Emmaus after a long day in Jerusalem and met a man on the road whom they thought was a stranger, but whom they soon discovered was really a friend. Along the road, these three people talked avidly about the day's events and their meaning in the light of Scripture. Later that evening the two residents of Emmaus finally recognized Jesus when he picked up the bread at the supper table, blessed it, broke it, and gave it to them (see Luke 24:30-31). They suddenly remembered that they'd been at a table with this friend before. With its clear reference to the original institution of the Lord's Supper (see 22:19), the story of Emmaus suggests that whenever we gather around the Lord's Table for communion, Christ is present, as close as an intimate friend.

Realizing who their companion really was, the two disciples said to each other, "Were not our hearts burning within us while he was talking to us on the road?" (24:32). A burning heart is a sign of true friendship. When I am with a close friend, my heart softly glows with affection and regard for my friend. A glowing, burning heart also happens to be one of the effects of contemplation. During contemplation, the intimate presence of Christ gently lights us on fire.

Paul further develops the theme of intimate friendship in his letters to the Corinthians and the Philippians. In 1 Corinthians, he describes us as the temple of God, where the Holy Spirit lives (see 3:16). Several chapters later, he asserts that "anyone united to the Lord becomes one spirit with him" (6:17). Paul later clarifies that this union with God is still in the process of being formed. Our transformation into God's light, love, and life happens gradually by degrees as we look at the glory of God. "And all of us, with unveiled faces, seeing the glory of the Lord as though reflected in a mirror, are being transformed into the same image from one degree of glory to another; for this comes from the Spirit" (2 Corinthians 3:18).

The biblical theme of friendship portrays the possibility of warm intimacy between us and God. Through our baptism, our practice of discipleship, and the gift of the dark night, the Holy Spirit transforms us so that we gradually enter into deeper levels of union with God. More and more we want what God wants, desire what God wills, and detect God's activities, consequently acting in ways that delight God. We see in a new way, think in a new way, behave in a new way. In response to the growing gift of contemplation our discipleship moves from "I must do these things to please a stern, demanding God" to "I want to do things for God out of gratitude and love." We become walking illustrations of Paul's insight that "it is no longer I who live, but it is Christ who lives in me" (Galatians 2:20).

The delights of new friendship with God more than compensate for our frustrations over God's apparent absence during the night. The new light of contemplation now shining in us more than makes up for the night's numbing darkness.

Friendship Within God

The source of our friendship with God is the friendship among the members of the Trinity. According to the medieval theologian Thomas Aquinas, Father, Son, and Holy Spirit have been best friends for all eternity. Before the creation of the world, the three persons of God already lived with each other in deep friendship. This community of three is where friendship first existed and where it achieves its fullest expression.[29]

The triune God shared this friendship with us in both the creation and the redemption of the world. In the creation of the world, God intended to live with us in intimate community. Although our sin marred God's original intention for intimacy with us and with the rest of creation, God did not give up the pursuit of friendship. We can read the Bible as the story of God's unending attempts to become friends with us once again, for in the gifts of liberation from bondage, of laws to order community, and of prophets to recall us to faithfulness, God tried to recreate friendship with us.

When these efforts to renew friendship proved less than satisfactory, God launched an even more dramatic initiative: God took on human form in Jesus and became like us so that we could find it easier to become friends with God. Jesus' teachings and healings are designed to enhance the friendship between us and God. When the resurrected Jesus breathed on the disciples and symbolically granted all believers the gift of the Holy Spirit (see John 20:22), friendship with God became even more possible. In a deep sense the mission of God is to produce a new friendship with us that God planned in the creation of the world, but lost because of our sin. The twin actions of incarnation and Pentecost—when one of the members of the Trinity came to earth—made the friendship within God available to us in a whole new way. Incarnation and Pentecost were God's efforts to share friendship with us.

Contemplation extends our friendship with God. In this life we will never enjoy the kind of friendship with God that the members of the Trinity enjoy with each other, even though their friendship remains our pattern. Yet through the gift of contemplation we can experience far greater heights of friendship with God than many of us imagine. No matter how good our friendship with God is, a more excellent friendship is always possible because there are, in God's grace, still new worlds of friendship for us to explore. Like the universe, which has no discernable boundaries, our friendship with God has no discernable limits.

Friendship with Creation

When we become more excellent friends with God, we also become more excellent friends with God's creation. We turn into better environmentalists because the dark night causes us to see God's creation in a whole new way. Prior to the dark night, most Christians see God reflected in the glory of a sunset on the beach, in the wonder of a rainbow after a storm, or in the majesty of snow-capped mountains set against a deep blue sky. We naturally glimpse something of God through God's creation.

After the growth of contemplation, the reverse can happen: we now see creation through God. We no longer only see God's presence in a grand oak tree, but we may also glimpse the oak tree through the eyes of God. When we gaze at a rose, we no longer think only of God, but instead gaze at the rose with "the mind of Christ" (1 Corinthians 2:16). The perspective from which we see things changes. Thanks to the inflow of God's love through contemplation, we no longer merely see things from "a human point of view" (2 Corinthians 5:16). We are steadily remade into a new creation (see 2 Corinthians 5:17). Through renewed eyes connected to a renewed mind (see Romans 12:2), we perceive that creation pulses with divine energy. Like God, we see that creation is "very good" (Genesis 1:31). Our passion heightens, honoring creation as the holy playground of God.

Freedom

Along with new friendship comes new freedom. Now that we are no longer so trapped by our own harmful attachments, we are freer to love others for who and what they are, rather than what we think they should be. The night begins to detach us from our false selves, freeing our true self to become friendlier with God, creation, and others.

Often we will first recognize this new freedom in our relationship with God. Painfully, we learn during the dark night that God is not bound by our assumptions or expectations and that God will do whatever God sees fit to do. God does not act during the dark night as we think God should act, which has the effect of sweeping our puny understandings of God aside. We squarely face the fact that God is not our servant but our sovereign. We realize that God sometimes acts contrary to our expectations, and from this we learn to let God be God.

Out of this experience with God we learn to extend the same freedom to other people, such as our colleagues at work, our spouse, or our children. Extending freedom to others comes in various forms. If I hoped to have a daughter who would grow up to be a family doctor, maybe I now realize that my daughter is turning out instead to be a potter. If I wanted my spouse to be athletic and join me in running a marathon or in riding a bicycle across the country, perhaps I now realize that she is happiest when sitting and reading books. She will never change, but I have learned to love her anyway. If I expected my business partner to go out and attract new customers, now I might see that his best gifts are really in managing our company's internal systems.

Similarly, we extend freedom to creation. We no longer need to dominate the natural world in quite the way we once may have. Instead of draining every swamp in order to grow corn, I learn that the biosphere needs wetlands for its overall health. Instead of forcing a river to stay in its channel by building levees, I realize after a flood that the river system functions much better if I lower the levees, let the river overflow into low-lying areas after a heavy rain, and refuse to construct buildings in those low areas. Instead of using artificial watering to grow temperate plants in semi-arid climates, I choose to plant native grasses, shrubs, and flowers well suited to the drier climate I live in.

The dark night frees us and unleashes us to free others. In this way it helps to reduce conflict and build peace between us and others. These changes tend to be gradual and incremental.

Sin After the Night

Can we still sin after emerging from a dark night? In this new friendship with God and others, can we still violate God's wishes? Yes. However, our attraction to sin has diminished because the Spirit, with our consent, is now closer to the surface of our awareness. We respond more readily to the Spirit's nudging. God is making progress in training us to accept heaven's promptings.

Where I live in northern Indiana, there are many Amish buggies and horses on the roads. I've noticed that the Amish generally do not hitch young, inexperienced, and skittish horses to their buggies when they want to drive on busy roads. Most of the horses pulling buggies along major roads are mature, settled, and well trained. They do not shy away, even from eighteen-wheeler trucks. These trained horses respond willingly to the driver's voice and to the signals the driver passes through the reins attached to the bit in the horse's mouth.

Only once have I seen a young, skittish horse pulling a buggy. Unaccustomed to fast vehicles with loud engines, this scared horse reared up on its hind legs and tried to run off into the field beside the road. Only with great difficulty did the man in the buggy manage to control the horse. Pulling hard on the reins, the man used a calm but commanding voice to direct the horse back onto the gravel berm between the asphalt road and the field. Seeing what was happening, I slowed my car to fifteen miles an hour and gave the man and his horse a wide berth. I realized that this horse had succumbed to its fear of noisy, speeding vehicles, that it had not yet learned to trust its owner. It needed more training so that it could respond obediently to the guidance its owner provided through reins, bridle, and bit.

Before the dark night, we're like a fearful, skittish horse. Even though we've been baptized, we easily succumb to sin because we're still in the early stages of learning how to trust and obey the Spirit's guidance. But as we emerge from the purgative training of the dark night, we're more like an experienced horse. We are more in tune with the Spirit and pay more attention to the Spirit's voice and signals. We are granted greater intimacy with the Spirit, as a mature horse and driver are intimate with each other after long experience of working together. In a tangible sense we and the Spirit are friends. As an owner cares deeply for the horse—giving it food and water, rubbing it down after a workout, and tending its ailments—so too does the Spirit care deeply for us. We know our owner's voice and trust that God is acting for our good. We increasingly go where the Spirit wants us to go and obey what the Spirit calls us to do. We can still go in a direction God doesn't want—and like a horse, we sometimes do—but this happens less often than before. After the dark night, we live in greater peace and unity with God.

—13—

COUNTERCULTURAL MISSION

So if anyone is in Christ, there is a new creation: everything old has passed away; see, everything has become new! All this is from God, who reconciled us to himself through Christ, and has given us the ministry of reconciliation; that is, in Christ God was reconciling the world to himself, not counting their trespasses against them, and entrusting the message of reconciliation to us. So we are ambassadors for Christ.
—2 Corinthians 5:17-20

A third transformation of the dark night is that it launches us into countercultural mission. Sometimes the night propels us to take up a different mission than we've had before; at other times the night sharpens our existing mission, defines it in a slightly different way or increases our dedication to it. A deeper commitment to mission is perhaps the most striking of all the conversions that can happen as a result of a dark night. While mission can be expressed in thousands of different ways, the essence of mission is always countercultural: by speech and example, we interpret God's alternate reality to the world.

For Paul this mission (or "ministry," 2 Corinthians 5:18) is related to God's work of reconciliation in the world. The purpose of contemplation is to create shalom in us, through us, and in the world. Although Paul did not write explicitly about the dark night, some sections of his letters, including the passage above, call to mind aspects of what Christians would later understand to be the dark night. After emerging from the night, we are closer to the new creation of being reconciled to God through Christ, of which a major mark is living a ministry of reconciliation in the world. To see the relationship between the dark night and countercultural mission, consider the story of Phoebe.

Phoebe

Phoebe, a single woman with three grown children, entered a dark night near the end of her youngest son's sophomore year at a nearby university and stayed in it for two more years. As God began to move her out of the night, she felt the urge for something new. Ever since her children were small, she had worked as a nurse in the emergency room of the local hospital, and while the pay was good and the work rewarding, the wish to do something more occupied her thoughts. She wondered whether she needed a change of location, a change in the type of nursing she was doing, or a change to another vocation.

One Sunday morning on her way to get a cup of coffee after the worship service, she strolled by the church's bulletin board that displayed mission opportunities, and a flyer caught her eye. She learned that her denomination's mission agency wanted a nurse to go to Botswana and work with AIDS patients and AIDS prevention for at least four years. "Intriguing," she thought to herself, "that's certainly something different, but it's not for me. I'd have to learn another language."

Yet the idea would not leave her. As she dozed on the sofa later that afternoon, images of working with AIDS patients flitted in front of her mind's eye. When she woke up, she turned on her computer and surfed the internet for articles on Botswana, just for fun. For the rest of the week the thought of nursing in Botswana hovered in and out of her consciousness. She tried to put it out of her mind—at her age, she really didn't want to learn another language—but the photos she had seen on the web kept sneaking back into her brain, especially one of a teenage Botswana woman with AIDS, lying in bed, attended by two of her aunts. The caption said the young woman's mother and father had already died of the disease. This photo and others like it made Phoebe realize that as awful as AIDS was in her hometown community, it was much worse in the developing world.

On the next Sunday morning, she went to the mission bulletin board and wrote down the contact information. That afternoon she wrote an email inquiring about the position. In two days she received a reply from the mission agency. Yes, the position was still open; yes, she would indeed have to learn Setswana, the native language. Attached to the email were a detailed job description and an application form in case she wanted to apply. Phoebe printed out both forms and laid them next to the candle on her prayer table as a kind of offering to God. Every morning and evening when she did centering prayer, the two papers were there, not as the focus of her praying but as a question for God: what shall I do with these?

She continued to discern by checking out books on Botswana from the public library and by consulting with her best friends and her small group. Should she apply, or shouldn't she? Could this be a call from God? She ate lunch with a couple in a neighboring town, who had lived in Botswana for a year. She debated the pros and cons with her children. After much conversation and prayer, she decided to apply and see what would happen. In a month, the mission agency invited her for an interview, during which Phoebe's interest in the position increased. A few days later the administrator at the agency who was responsible for Africa phoned and offered her the position. By then it was clear to Phoebe that she wanted to do this, language study and all. It felt like a call from God, and she accepted.

Five months later Phoebe moved to Botswana. After six months of language study in the capital city of Gaborone, she moved to a cluster of villages on the edge of the Kalahari Desert to care for patients and to teach AIDS prevention. There she faced the normal challenges of adjusting to a new culture and to different medical standards. She worked diligently at forming relationships with villagers and patients. As best as she could, she tried to adjust to being far away from her children and friends.

Perhaps the most significant struggle was finding new and workable patterns of prayer. At home in Ontario her favorite season had been winter, when the subtle loveliness of snow sent her into a contemplative spirit. Botswana, of course, had no snow at all. "How can I pray on the edge of the desert?" she wondered. "I know in my head that the Spirit is here too, but how do I connect emotionally with God in this place? What in this landscape communicates to me the beauty of creation and of the God who made it?"

After some experimenting, she discovered that the best time to pray was just before sunrise, when the air was coolest and life was starting to stir in the village. The sun's morning rays surrounding her hut became a symbol for the light of God enveloping her. In odd moments during the day when she wasn't busy working and developing friendships in the village, she carefully paid attention to local plant and animal life. This contemplative seeing became an additional way to pray. In the red sand, in the subtle shades of green plants, and in the vertical leaps of springbok, she found beauty for the simple reason that God had made them.

At the end of her third year in Botswana, Phoebe wrote an Easter letter to her friends back home in which she reflected on her sense of mission.

In these three years I've befriended hundreds of people with AIDS. I've also witnessed the death of dozens of them: the gradual physical wasting, the unstoppable weakening of body and spirit, the abandonment by some extended family members, and finally the slow sinking into death. AIDS is a democratic disease, striking rich and poor, female and male, old and young, Christians and non-Christians. And quite a few of those who get AIDS have not themselves engaged in promiscuous behavior. Instead they get it from the unhygienic handling of body fluids, or from philandering husbands, or from their mother while still in the womb. I realize now, even more than when I first arrived in Botswana, that this work could kill me. One slip of a hypodermic needle, one sloppy medical procedure, one unattended cut, and the HIV virus could enter my own bloodstream, multiply in my body, make me sick, and some day, kill me. The chances of it happening are small, but they do exist.

Yet I am not afraid. In a sense, it no longer matters whether I live or die. I've finished raising my three children and somehow each of them will have to find his or her own way in the world. Even if I live to be 90, they will still have to find their own way. Moreover, I've already had a full and rich life. I don't mean rich in material possessions, although certainly in Canada my life was comfortable enough. Even though here in Botswana my life is stripped down to just a handful of possessions, I have all I really need. What I mean by "a full and rich life" is that I've already had many good times in the course of my life and that I've done my best to savor those times in gratitude to God. I've eaten lots of great food, worked fulfilling jobs, had wonderful friends, belonged to healthy congregations, served others for the sake of Christ, and worshiped an incomparable God. And now I live in a country among a people I've come to love. I cannot imagine anything in life better than what I've already experienced. What more do I need out of life? Nothing, really. I am satisfied.

Mind you, I'm not saying I want to die. But I am saying I'm ready to die. If I'm murdered, die in a traffic accident, get AIDS, or go out in any of dozens of other nasty ways, it will be ok. I will be ok, because I know beyond question that I belong to Christ, and that the One who raised Jesus from death will somehow also take care of me when I die. I still try to be safe, of course; but I know only too well that this work in Botswana is inherently risky, partly because medical standards aren't as rigorous as they are in Canada.

The itch that I felt over three and a half years ago for something more has been scratched. This is the work that God wants me to do now. Therefore I've just signed on to another term of service, this time for five more years. At the end of the summer I'll return to Ontario for a short furlough to visit all of you. But this place, these people, and this ministry are where I belong. In a sense, this is my new home.

Radical Trust

Phoebe's letter to friends in Canada conveys a radical trust in God—not a trust that God will keep death away, but that God's presence and power surpass death. Having passed through a dark night, Phoebe's inward life of prayer continues throughout the day. Caring for patients, cooking and eating, and laughing with villagers are as prayerful for her as the thirty minutes of focused contemplative prayer at dawn.

A nearly continual awareness of God in the wake of a dark night is one of the chief reasons that the night hones our counter-cultural edge. When we are grounded in God, we more readily risk living in odd, unconventional ways. Instead of pursuing wealth, fame, or power, we more willingly pursue service to others in obedience to Christ. Knowing that we and God are friends, we become countercultural. We are free to think, act, and speak in ways unlike most other people do. God has decentered our self-love and recentered us in God, our profoundest center. We can therefore be courageously different.

Less Afraid of Dying

Another way Phoebe demonstrates courageous living is how she approaches death. North American culture is full of people who are afraid to die. Particularly in the United States, we spend huge amounts of healthcare dollars on extreme measures near the end of life. We try to push off the day of our death as long as possible, even if by only a few weeks or months. I've watched some Christians fight their own death with every available medical technology, regardless of the financial cost. I've witnessed obviously dying Christians blithely spend money on themselves as if they were going to live for another twenty years. And when they can no longer deny to themselves they will soon die, I've watched fear creep into their eyes.

By contrast, people who have been through a dark night more often approach death with open arms, trusting in the depth of their spirits that Christ awaits them on the other side. They may reject measures to prolong life as long as possible. Quite simply, they are not afraid to die, and once they are no longer afraid to die, they are free to live in unusual ways. Phoebe accepts the possibility of dying as a result of caring for people with AIDS. In a context where people with AIDS are sometimes abandoned, Phoebe's care for the dying is a visible expression of God's reconciling love.

Varieties of Countercultural Mission

Phoebe illustrates only one way God can point us to some form of countercultural mission after a dark night. There are many others. I have seen people

- develop a more radical commitment to living with the poor;
- become foster parents;
- sharply critique our acquisitive consumer economy and sell off, or give away, their own superfluous possessions;
- leave high-paying, high-status jobs to take lower-income assignments that allow them to serve others more directly;

- leave secular professions to become pastors or church workers;
- reject violence and the evil of military power on which it depends;
- place complete trust in God, arguing that Christians have no need for national security;
- question our culture's frenetic, fast-paced lifestyle, saying no to busyness in order to live slower and more serenely;
- work tirelessly for environmental conservation;
- refuse to do any work on the Sabbath, but rest as God intended;
- ride bicycles instead of driving cars, use rakes instead of leaf blowers, and shovel snow instead of buying snow blowers;
- love enemies in astonishing ways;
- forgive people who abused them;
- nurture deeper faith in other people through spiritual writing and spiritual guidance;
- reject the ceaseless competition to be first, best, strongest, fastest, or most famous, and instead become content with the being the last, the worst, the weakest, the slowest, or least well known.

Countercultural mission typically becomes an inner driving force that will not let us go. It demands to be lived. We feel that we cannot refuse this mission. We spend a lot of time thinking and daydreaming about it. It frolics in our mind, makes our heart beat faster, and becomes our central passion, even in the face of stiff opposition.

A Fruit of Contemplation

Contemplation births countercultural mission. In earlier chapters I noted that contemplation is loving, gentle, peaceful, and gracious. But contemplation also needs to go somewhere and result in something; it is not just for itself. Contemplation has not achieved its full purpose if it only stays inside us as a nice experience. When we continue to welcome God's gift of contemplation, the Holy Spirit will express the fruit of contemplation in our worldview and in the way we live (see Galatians 5:22-23).

The urge for countercultural mission begins to stir in most people within months after God's contemplation begins to flow. Sometimes, like Phoebe, we soon afterward find ourselves in the middle of a mission that we did not previously imagine. Expressing our countercultural mission may not always happen this soon, however. As we emerge from the dark night, the outlines of this mission may still be a little unclear in our minds. Even if the mission is clear, it may not yet be obvious how to carry it out. Our culture wants instant results, but quickness is not necessarily God's way. God, after all, has forever to accomplish things. A vision for a new, deeper mission might build in us for several years before we are actually ready to do it. We might need further training or certification before we can carry out what God is calling us to do. Even if the vision is well shaped in our minds and we already have the skills to carry it out, the context may not be quite right yet. We may be called to watch and pray for a while until the situation changes and God says, "Do it now!"

A Countercultural Process

Contemplation leads to countercultural mission partly because contemplation itself is a countercultural process. In a culture of busyness that admires efficient people who work excessively long hours and produce a long list of tangible results, contemplation looks suspiciously like wasting time. Someone who sits on a stool, staring out the window, appears to be doing nothing at all—at least nothing useful and productive. Yet while staring out the window the person might be receiving God's loving, peaceful inflow. People with their eyes closed at least look like they're praying, but some contemplation happens with our eyes open. Others may question whether the act of sitting, looking, and being really contributes to holiness. And yet it may be one of the holiest things we do.

Still, much contemplation does happen with our eyes closed, especially during centering prayer, which is peculiarly adept at inviting the inflow of God's love. If every morning and every afternoon we practice twenty minutes of centering prayer, we are quite countercultural. Who in our culture besides religious people would "waste" forty minutes a day in silence? Even for many Christians, contemplation runs counter to the usual understanding of prayer. The only kind of worthwhile prayer, we suppose, is prayer in which we work hard to find the right words to make God feel good (praise) or to persuade God to do what we want (petition and intercession). If we have a more activist spirituality, we might think that real prayer is finding the right deeds to make God pleased with us. Praise, petition, intercession, and service are legitimate forms of prayer, of course. But contemplation, based on quietly receiving whatever God wants to give us, looks and feels like a markedly different way of praying. For some people it doesn't feel like prayer at all.

For all that, contemplation is an extremely important way to pray. Each time divine love flows into us during contemplation, the Holy Spirit reconciles us a little more to God. Slowly we become more like God, transformed in the image of Christ. Because Christ's way is counter to every human way, the prayerful process of contemplation changes us into God's countercultural ambassadors of mission. In this way God's gift of contemplation, itself a countercultural process, naturally propels us into countercultural mission.

A Closing Image

I end with an image. One winter afternoon as I worked in my study, a light snow began to fall. Since winter had been unusually mild so far and we hadn't seen any snow for weeks, this snowfall was a welcome sight. As dusk turned into the darkness of night, the snow still fell, yet it didn't seem to make much difference: the world continued to look drab. Many of these first flakes melted within seconds after they landed.

I was astonished, however, when I woke up the next morning, for the snow had transformed the world outside my window. Snowing all night, millions upon millions of flakes had descended from the sky into the arms of a waiting earth. I pulled on warm clothes and went outside to investigate. On the crabapple tree in the front yard, snowflakes had gathered one by one on the top side of the branches, and then around the edges and down the sides, until each branch bore as much snow as it possibly could. In the back yard, snow spread across the limbs of the blue spruce like a blanket.

As far as I could see in every direction, the world was made new. Without any effort from the earth except a willingness to receive, the gift of snow, falling silently all night long, had slowly but surely transformed the world.

So too are we re-created by the manna of contemplation.

FOR FURTHER READING

Bourgeault, Cynthia. *Centering Prayer and Inner Awakening.* Cambridge: Cowley Publications, 2004.

Cronk, Sandra. *Dark Night Journey: Inward Re-patterning Toward a Life Centered in God.* Wallingford, Pa.: Pendle Hill Publications, 1991.

Egan, Keith J., ed. *Carmelite Prayer: A Tradition for the 21st Century.* Mahwah, N.J.: Paulist Press, 2003.

Fitzgerald, Constance. "Impasse and Dark Night." In *Living with Apocalypse: Spiritual Resources for Social Compassion.* Edited by Tilden H. Edwards. San Francisco: Harper & Row, 1984.

Green, Thomas H. *When the Well Runs Dry: Prayer Beyond the Beginnings,* rev. ed. Notre Dame: Ave Maria, 1998.

John of the Cross. *The Collected Works of St. John of the Cross,* rev. ed. Translated by Kieran Kavanaugh and Otilio Rodriguez. Washington, D.C.: Institute of Carmelite Studies, 1991.

Johnston, William, ed. *The Cloud of Unknowing and The Book of Privy Counseling.* New York: Image/Doubleday, 1973, 1996.

Keating, Thomas. *Open Mind, Open Heart: The Contemplative Dimension of the Gospel.* New York: Continuum, 1986, 1992.

Laird, Martin. *Into the Silent Land: A Guide to the Christian*

Practice of Contemplation. Oxford: Oxford University Press, 2006.

Matthew, Iain. *The Impact of God: Soundings from St. John of the Cross*. London: Hodder & Stoughton, 1994.

May, Gerald G. *The Dark Night of the Soul: A Psychiatrist Explores the Connection Between Darkness and Spiritual Growth*. San Francisco: HarperSanFrancisco, 2004.

Merton, Thomas. *Contemplative Prayer*. Garden City, N.Y.: Image Books, 1969.

————. *The Inner Experience: Notes on Contemplation*. Edited by William H. Shannon. San Francisco: HarperSanFrancisco, 2004.

Mother Teresa. *Mother Teresa: Come Be My Light*. Edited by Brian Kolodiejchuk. New York: Doubleday, 2007.

Nouwen, Henri. *The Inner Voice of Love: A Journey Through Anguish to Freedom*. New York: Image/Doubleday, 1994.

Teresa of Avila. *The Book of Her Life*. Vol. 1 of *The Collected Works of St. Teresa of Avila*, 2nd ed. Translated by Kieran Kavanaugh and Otilio Rodriguez. Washington, D.C.: ICS Publications, 1987.

Teresa of Avila. *The Interior Castle*. Vol. 2 of *The Collected Works of St. Teresa of Avila*. Translated by Kieran Kavanaugh and Otilio Rodriguez. Washington, D.C.: ICS Publications, 1987.

Turner, Denys. *The Darkness of God: Negativity in Christian Mysticism*. Cambridge: Cambridge University Press, 1995.

NOTES

1. Thomas Merton, *Contemplative Prayer* (Garden City, N.Y.: Image, 1971), 38, 43-44.

2. When people in the English-speaking world talk about the dark night, they commonly call it "the dark night of the soul." But John of the Cross never used the Spanish equivalent, *la noche oscura del alma*, in his writings. In deference to his preferred phrase *la noche oscura*, I use "the dark night" in this book.

3. The Spanish word *oscura* can mean both "dark" and "obscure." In line with tradition, I use *dark night* in this book, since the phrase has virtually become a technical term in Christian spiritual theology. Yet after carefully examining all John's uses of *oscura, oscuras, oscuro, oscurida*d, and forms of the verb *oscurecer*, I believe a case can be made in favor of translating *la noche oscura* as "the obscure night." As well as being consistent with John's usage, "obscure night" picks up an important theme that most people I have interviewed about their experience of the night articulate: their sense that the night is obscure and confusing. They typically do not understand what is happening to them, why it is happening, or how to respond to it. "Obscure" may be more apt than "dark."

4. John writes about these signs in four different places, listing them in a different order and using slightly different language. I have worded these as simply as I can. See *The Sayings of Light and Love*, no. 119, *The Ascent of Mount Carmel* (2.13.2-4), *The Dark Night* (1.9.2-3, 8), and *The*

Living Flame of Love (3.32-33) in Kieran Kavanaugh and Otilio Rodriguez, trans., *The Collected Works of St. John of the Cross*, rev. ed. (Washington, D.C.: Institute of Carmelite Studies, 1991).

5. In the Old Testament, see Genesis 1:1-5; 15:1-21; 28:10-22; 32:22-31; Exodus 12:1-51; 14:10-31; Ruth 3:1-18; 4:17; 1 Samuel 3:1-21; Jonah 1:17–2:10. In the New Testament, see Matthew 25:1-13; 26:20-29, 36-75; 27:45-61; 28:1-10; Mark 1:32-34; Luke 2:1-20; John 3:1-21; 6:16-21; 13:1-15; 17:1-26; Acts 9:1-9; 16:25-34.

6. For this point, I am indebted to Keith J. Egan in a conversation on April 29, 2005.

7. *The Dark Night*, 2.1.1.

8. Thomas Keating, *Invitation to Love: The Way of Christian Contemplation* (New York: Continuum, 1992), 99-100.

9. *The Dark Night*, 1.4.2, 2.3.1; *The Spiritual Canticle*, 13.4; *The Living Flame of Love*, 3.2.

10. The manual I used actually reads, "Are you willing to give and receive counsel in the congregation?" I modified this question at Thomas's baptism to reflect the fact that he needed to flee immediately afterward and would not be able to stay in the congregation I was pastoring. See John Rempel, ed., *Minister's Manual* (Newton, Kan.: Faith & Life Press, 1998), p. 48.

11. In addition to the stories I tell about myself in this book, the story of Thomas actually did happen as written.

12. For more on the false self and true self, and their role in Christian spiritual development, see Thomas Keating, *Intimacy with God* (New York: Crossroad, 1994), 72-91.

13. People in Christian history have used the words *meditation* and *contemplation* in somewhat different ways, depending on their theological perspectives and historical circumstances. I have tried to describe them in a way that honors the tradition while also being clear about what I mean by these words. However, the distinction between meditation and contemplation is not always clear in the lives of real people, since some spiritual practices, such as centering prayer, operate somewhere between what we might call "pure" meditation and "pure" contemplation. During a given period of prayer, it's also quite possible for us to alternate between meditation and contemplation. Perhaps we could imagine meditation

and contemplation as two different points along a continuum; our spiritual life and our particular spiritual practices flow back and forth along the continuum in response to God's initiatives and our own needs and desires. The dark night marks a movement away from meditation (perhaps without entirely leaving it) and toward contemplation.

14. For more on the problem of attachments, see John of the Cross, *The Ascent of Mount Carmel*, Book One; and *The Dark Night*, 1.1-7.

15. For more on Taizé prayer, see www.taize.fr/en.

16. For more on centering prayer, visit the website of Contemplative Outreach at www.contemplativeoutreach.org/frntpage.htm. The mission of this international ecumenical organization is to help ordinary Christians practice centering prayer.

17. Many websites have information about building and praying with labyrinths. A good one is www.labyrinth-enterprises.com/index.html.

18. More about lectio divina is available on the Contemplative Outreach website at http://www.contemplativeoutreach.org/lectio/lectio.htm, or by typing *lectio divina* into your favorite internet search engine.

19. See Mother Teresa, *Mother Teresa: Come Be My Light*, ed. Brian Kolodiejchuk (New York: Doubleday, 2007).

20. I thank Dave Miller for this insight.

21. A list of Mennonite spiritual directors is available at http://www.mennoniteusa.org/Portals/0/WebDownloads/DM/Spiritual -Directors.pdf. If none of these are in your area or if you do not want a Mennonite, look for other Christian guides near you. The best source on the internet is the website of Spiritual Directors International, located at www.sdiworld.org/seekfindguide.html. Each person on these two lists has been trained in the art of spiritual direction and is committed to abide by certain ethical standards. Some large cities also have an ecumenical network of spiritual directors that you can find in the phone book. If you are comfortable with computers, consider the possibility of receiving spiritual direction over the internet using a webcam and a headset. A few spiritual directors in North America and elsewhere have recently started to offer this service. You can search the internet for possibilities.

22. Gerald G. May, *The Dark Night of the Soul: A Psychiatrist Explores the Connection Between Darkness and Spiritual Growth* (San Francisco: HarperSanFrancisco, 2004), 155-59.

23. Kevin Culligan, "The Dark Night and Depression," in *Carmelite Prayer: A Tradition for the 21st Century*, ed. Keith J. Egan (Mahwah, N.J.: Paulist Press, 2003), 119-38.

24. "Symptoms of Depression," http://www.dbsalliance.org/ site/PageServer?pagename=Signs_symptoms, accessed on October 18, 2008. The National Institute of Mental Health has published a pamphlet on depression, available at http://www.nimh.nih.gov/health/ publications/depression/nimhdepression.pdf, accessed October 18, 2008.

25. For this chart, I have also used May's earlier book *Care of Mind/Care of Spirit: A Psychiatrist Explores Spiritual Direction* (San Francisco: HarperSanFrancisco, 1992), 102-12.

26. See David Emmanuel Goatley, *Were You There? Godforsakenness in Slave Religion* (Maryknoll, N.Y.: Orbis, 1996).

27. See Constance Fitzgerald, "Impasse and Dark Night," in *Living with Apocalypse: Spiritual Resources for Social Compassion*, ed. Tilden H. Edwards (San Francisco: Harper & Row, 1984), 93-116.

28. Teresa of Avila, *The Book of Her Life*, 8.5, in *The Collected Works of St. Teresa of Avila*, vol. 1, trans. Kieran Kavanaugh and Otilio Rodriguez, 2nd ed. (Washington, D.C.: ICS Publications, 1987).

29. Lawrence S. Cunningham and Keith J. Egan, *Christian Spirituality: Themes from the Tradition* (Mahwah, N.J.: Paulist Press, 1996), 173-74.

THE AUTHOR

Daniel P. Schrock has been a pastor at Berkey Avenue Mennonite Fellowship in Goshen, Indiana, since 2002 and previously served in urban ministry in Miami, Chicago, and Columbus, Ohio. He also works as a spiritual director and is president of Dan Schrock Spiritual Direction. He holds a doctor of ministry in Christian spirituality from Col-  umbia Theological Seminary and a master's in theology from Chicago Theological Seminary. He has written articles and reviews in many journals and has authored and taught curriculum on Scripture and spiritual direction. Schrock was born in Elkhart, Indiana. He lives in Goshen with his wife, Jennifer, and their two sons, Peter and Nicholas.